Fresh Herb *Chicken*

Melt 1 tablespoon margarine or butter in 12-inch non-stick skillet over medium heat. Add chicken and brown on each side. Add 1/4 cup dry white wine or chicken broth, 2 tablespoons chopped fresh basil, dill or chives and 1/4 teaspoon salt. Cook about 8 minutes, turning once, or until chicken is no longer pink in center.

Caesar Chicken with *Feta*

Heat 1/4 cup Caesar dressing (not creamy type) in 12-inch nonstick skillet over medium heat. Add chicken and cook about 10 minutes, turning once, or until chicken is no longer pink in center.

A few minutes before removing from heat, sprinkle chicken with 1 cut-up tomato and 1/2 cup crumbled feta cheese; cover skillet to soften cheese.

Ranch *Chicken*

Heat 2 tablespoons oil in 12-inch nonstick skillet over medium heat. Dip chicken into 1/4 cup ranch dressing, then coat with 1/3 cup dry Italian-style or seasoned bread crumbs. Cook about 10 minutes, turning once, or until chicken is no longer pink in center.

Italian Chicken and *Peppers*

Heat 1/4 cup Italian dressing (not creamy type) in 12-inch nonstick skillet over medium heat. Add chicken and cook about 10 minutes, turning once, or until chicken is no longer pink in center.

During last 5 minutes of cooking, add 2 small bell peppers, cut into strips, stirring once or twice.

Quick Main Dish Chicken Salads

These wonderfully speedy salads are made easily by getting a jump start from ready-to-eat bags of lettuce and vegetable mixtures or complete salad mixes, which contain dressing, croutons and sometimes cheese. These timesaving products can be found in the produce section of the supermarket. Follow directions below for great greens anytime.

Oriental *Chicken Salad*

Prepare 1 bag complete Oriental salad mix as directed on bag, dividing into 4 individual servings.

Top each salad with about 1/2 cup cut-up cooked chicken and canned mandarin orange segments.

Broccoli-Peanut *Chicken Salad*

Mix 4 cups broccoli slaw (from a 16 ounce bag) with 2 cups cut cooked chicken and 1/3 to 1/2 cup peanut sauce.

Sprinkle with chopped peanuts and cilantro leaves.

Raspberry *Chicken Salad*

Prepare 1 bag complete raspberry Romaine salad mix as directed on bag, dividing into 4 individual servings.

Top each salad with a grilled chicken breast, cut into strips, fresh raspberries and toasted slivered almonds.

Chicken and *Swiss Salad*

Mix 4 cups broccoli slaw (from a 16 ounce bag) with 1 cup cut-up chicken, 1 cup shredded Swiss cheese, 1/2 cup dried cranberries or raisins and 1/2 cup coleslaw or ranch dressing.

Sprinkle with sunflower nuts and garnish with sliced red onion.

Southwest *Salad*

Mix together 1 cup cut-up cooked chicken and 1 cup salsa in large bowl. Add 6 cups iceberg lettuce salad mix (from a 16 ounce bag), 1 cup shredded Cheddar cheese, 1 can corn with red and green peppers (drained) and 1 small can sliced ripe olives (drained).

Toss to coat. Add 2 cups corn chips; toss to combine. Serve with additional salsa.

Betty Crocker's

Best Chicken

COOKBOOK

Chicken Fricassee
(page 168)

Betty Crocker's
Best Chicken
COOKBOOK

Macmillan • USA

MACMILLAN GENERAL REFERENCE USA

A Pearson Education Macmillan Company

1633 Broadway

New York, NY 10019-6785

Macmillan Publishing books may be purchased for business or sales promotional use. For information please write: Special Markets Department, Macmillan Publishing USA, 1633 Broadway, New York, NY 10019.

Library of Congress Cataloging-in-Publication Data

Crocker, Betty
  [Best Chicken Cookbook]
  Betty Crocker's Best Chicken Cookbook.
    p. cm.
  ISBN: 0-02-863155-2 (alk. paper)
    Cookery (Chicken) 2. Cookery (Turkey) I. Title.
TX750.5.C45C747   1999
641.6'65—dc21   99-17883
                                         CIP

GENERAL MILLS, INC.

Betty Crocker Kitchens
Manager, Publishing: Lois L. Tlusty

Editor: Lori Fox

Recipe Development: Julie Turnbull
Food Stylists: Carol Grones, Mary Johnson, Judy Tills
Nutritionists: Nancy Holmes, R.D.

Photographic Services:
Art Director: Emily Oberg
Photographer: Steven B. Olson

For consistent baking results, the Betty Crocker Kitchens recommend Gold Medal Flour.

Front cover photo: Chicken Marsala, page 160
Flap photo: Vegetable Chicken Stir-fry, page 32
Back cover top: Chili-Rubbed Chicken, page 192
Back cover bottom: Crunchy Oven-fried Chicken, page 156

Manufactured in the United States of America

10 9 8 7 6 5 4 3

First Edition

Contents

Spicy Chicken and Broccoli (page 71)

All about Chicken

Types of Chicken

Everyone loves chicken! And what isn't to love about it? It can be fixed any which way you choose—roasted to a turn, fried to a crisp, tucked into soups or sandwiches, stir-fried, to a creamed, stuffed, grilled or slowly simmered. You'll never run out of things to do with chicken. And if it's flavor you're after, chicken is friendly toward just about any seasoning; from hot and spicy to cool and fruity, you can make it any way you want. It's so versatile that it earns an "A" for cooperation in the kitchen. The only thing that might ruffle your feathers is trying to decide what type of chicken to buy. Do you find it tough to choose? Do you find it puzzling to decide between a fryer or a roaster, a free range or Amish chicken, frozen or fresh? We're here to help.

Birds of a Feather

Listed below are some facts about various types of chicken you'll find in the supermarket, plus information on the different ways chickens are raised.

BROILER-FRYER CHICKENS: This all-purpose chicken weighs from 3 to 3 1/2 pounds; the best bargain is the whole bird. Larger birds will have a higher ratio of meat to bone. Allow about 3/4 pound (bone-in) per serving.

ROASTER CHICKENS: This chicken is larger than the broiler-fryer chicken, weighing 4 to 6 pounds. Yet despite their larger size and longer cooking time, they are still tender and stay moist.

STEWING CHICKENS: This chicken (also referred to as a hen) weighs 4 1/2 to 6 pounds and provides a generous amount of meat. It is mature so it is not as tender as the roaster or broiler-fryer, but it's a very flavorful bird and is best used in stew and soup recipes.

ROCK CORNISH HENS: These small, specially bred chickens (also referred to as game hens) weigh 1 to 1 1/2 pounds and have only white meat. Allow one-half to a whole hen per person. Look for these hens in the grocery freezer case.

Raising Chickens

Most chickens in your local supermarket are commercially raised; however, if you purchase your chickens from farmers' markets, butchers or specialty food stores, you may see these different types of chicken. Some people believe that raising chickens by these methods gives you a more flavorful bird in the end. Read on to find out more.

AMISH CHICKENS: Amish chickens are raised on farms in Amish and Mennonite areas, mainly in east central Ohio and northern Indiana, using "old-fashioned" methods. Chickens are fed from hanging baskets inside large barns where they can roam. The feed comes from local co-ops and is tested for pesticides and insecticides. The chickens are not given hormones or any other growth-stimulation drugs. They are given antibiotics only when necessary at two weeks old (antibiotics stay in the bodies of chickens for two weeks). The chickens are processed when they are seven weeks old, and they are slightly smaller than some in the industry. Due to the type of feed and methods used in raising, these chickens have whiter skin than chickens from commercial processors. Some people believe that these chickens are moister and have a fresher flavor than commercial chickens.

FREE-RANGE CHICKENS: The term "free-range" describes a method of raising poultry whereby animals are allowed to roam and have access to pasture. In contrast to mass-produced birds, free-range chickens are raised in portable houses or pens that are moved regularly, so the chickens can forage for a variety of food such as grass and seeds.

There are two popular methods for raising free-range chickens. In the first method, long, portable houses, holding up to 400 chickens, are towed by tractor every few weeks to new locations in the pasture. These houses are enclosed in chicken wire with tarp-covered roofs and doors on both ends. The chickens are allowed out of these houses during the day, and the chickens usually stay within 100 feet.

The other popular method uses bottomless pens that are moved daily to fresh pasture. From 75 to 100 chickens are placed in these pens, where feed and water are available. The chickens are allowed to forage on plants, seeds, insects and worms. Most free-range farms are relatively small, with between 5,000 and 8,000 birds. Because these chickens are allowed to roam and to eat not only feed but also grass, plants and seeds, some people believe that they are moister and tastier than commercial chickens. There are no government standards for free-range chicken.

KOSHER CHICKENS: The word kosher generally refers to Jewish dietary laws. Kosher products are sanctioned by stringent Jewish law to adhere to specific preparation, so a food labeled as kosher means that it is acceptable to eat according to this law. Chicken processed according to kosher guidelines is given a symbol, U, indicating that the laws have been followed and the product does not contain any nonkosher ingredients. Another symbol is the K, which also stands for kosher. Kosher chickens generally taste a bit saltier than conventional chicken because salting the bird is part of the koshering process.

ORGANIC CHICKENS: The term organic refers to "earth-friendly" methods for growing and processing foods. These chickens are not given hormones or antibiotics, and they are fed organic feed, which is free from pesticides, by-products and growth stimulators.

A food labeled "certified organic" means that the farm has been inspected and found to comply with the guidelines below, developed by an organization of organic farmers:

1. No harmful chemicals have been applied to soil or products for at least three years.

2. The farmer and processor have annual certified inspections.

3. The farmer and processor have kept detailed records of their practices.

4. The farmer uses ecologically friendly methods and substances to control pests and enrich the soil.

An organic chicken is generally thinner and yellower, and has less fat and more flavor than conventional chicken. Many organic chickens are also free-range.

How Do I Buy Great Chicken or Turkey?

Choosing the freshest poultry available is easy if you use these tips:

Label and Package
- Check the sell-by date on the label (product dating is not a federal requirement). This shows the last day the product should be sold, but the product will still be fresh if prepared and eaten within two days of this date.
- Package trays or bags should have very little or no liquid in the bottom.
- Avoid torn and leaking packages.
- Avoid packages that are stacked in the refrigerator case too high. They may not be cold enough, which shortens shelf life.
- Frozen poultry should be hard to the touch and free of freezer burn.

Odor and Appearance
- Check for a fresh odor. Off odors can usually be smelled through the plastic, so if you smell something unusual, the product is not fresh.
- Select whole birds and cut-up pieces that are plump and meaty with smooth, moist-looking skin.

- Skinless, boneless products should look plump and moist.

- The color of chicken skin doesn't indicate quality. Skin color can range from yellow to white, depending on what the chicken was fed. Turkey, however, should have cream-colored skin.

- The cut ends of the poultry bones should be pink to red in color; if they are gray, the bird is not as fresh.

- Avoid poultry with traces of feathers. It may not have been handled properly, and the feathers don't add anything to a cooked dish!

Handling Poultry While Shopping

- Avoid contamination of grocery-cart contents! Place poultry in plastic bags, and put them in a part of the shopping cart so that any bacteria that may be present in the juices does not drip on and contaminate other foods, especially those that will be eaten without further cooking.

Poultry Storage

In the Fridge

UNCOOKED POULTRY: Refrigerate raw poultry no longer than two days. Store tray-packed products and whole products packaged in bags in their original wrapping in the coldest part of refrigerator (40° or below). Rewrap chicken that is wrapped in meat-market paper before storing it. First, rinse the poultry with cold water, then pat dry with paper towels and repackage in either heavy-duty plastic bags, several layers of plastic wrap (place poultry in a dish or baking pan with sides to prevent leakage on refrigerator shelves during storage) or food storage containers with tight-fitting lids.

COOKED POULTRY: Cover or wrap cooked poultry tightly and refrigerate no longer than two days. Be sure to reheat leftovers thoroughly. Keep leftovers moist while reheating by covering them; covering also will ensure that they are thoroughly heated in the center.

CHICKEN FIXINGS: Remove all stuffing from the bird cavity before refrigerating. Store leftover cooked stuffing up to three to four days and gravy one to two days. Place any cooked giblets, stuffing and gravy in sep-

arate containers to store in refrigerator. Before serving leftover gravies and marinades, bring them to a rolling boil and boil 1 minute.

In the Freezer

UNCOOKED POULTRY: Freeze cut-up and boneless chicken and turkey for up to nine months, whole chicken and turkey for up to twelve months. Wrap the poultry tightly in moisture- and vapor-resistant freezer wrap, heavy-duty plastic freezer bags or heavy-duty aluminum foil. Store giblets separately. Press as much air as possible out of the package before sealing it to prevent ice crystals from forming and freezer burn. Mark the package with the date and contents before freezing.

COOKED POULTRY: Wrap tightly in moisture- and vapor-resistant freezer wrap, heavy-duty plastic freezer bags or heavy-duty aluminum foil, and freeze for up to one month. Store poultry, giblets, stuffing and gravy in separate containers. Mark the package with the date and contents before freezing.

Thawing

UNCOOKED POULTRY: Thaw frozen uncooked chicken or turkey gradually in your refrigerator, never at room temperature on your countertop because that temperature provides the perfect environment for bacteria to grow. Place poultry in a dish or baking pan with sides to prevent leakage on refrigerator shelves during thawing.

How Long Will Poultry Take to Thaw in the Fridge?

- **Whole Chicken:** Allow 24 hours for a 3- to 4-pound chicken.

- **Whole Turkey:** Allow 24 hours for each 5 pounds, or use this timetable:

  1 to 2 days for 8 to 12 pounds

  2 to 3 days for 12 to 16 pounds

  3 to 4 days for 16 to 20 pounds

  4 to 5 days for 20 to 24 pounds

- **Cut-Up Chicken or Turkey Pieces:** Allow 3 to 9 hours for pieces.

How to Flatten Chicken Breasts

All it takes is a little bit of muscle to flatten chicken breasts until they're about 1/4 inch thick. Because they are thinner, chicken breasts or thighs can be used for fast, easy recipes such as Chicken-Pesto Sandwiches (page 250) and Lemon-Pistachio Chicken (page 92). The flat, even shape is perfect for more elegant recipes that are rolled up with a filling, such as Oven Chicken Kiev (page 154). It's easy to do using one of our methods below.

1. Place chicken breast between pieces of plastic wrap or waxed paper. Using flat side of meat mallet, pounder or a rolling pin, gently pound chicken breasts until they are 1/4 inch thick.

2. Place chicken breast between pieces of plastic wrap or waxed paper. Using heel of your hand, apply firm pressure (pounding lightly, if necessary) to chicken breasts, pressing until they are 1/4 inch thick.

Fast Thawing Guidelines

- **Cold Water Method:** Frozen uncooked chicken and turkey can also be safely thawed in cold water only. For food safety reasons do not use warm or hot water. Place poultry in its original wrap or in a resealable, heavy-duty plastic bag in cold water. Allow 30 minutes per pound to thaw, and change the water often to make sure it stays cold. If you're not going to use the poultry immediately, store it in the refrigerator as directed above; do not refreeze.

- **Microwave Method:** Frozen uncooked and cooked poultry can be thawed in the microwave oven following the manufacturer's directions.

How to Thinly Slice Raw Poultry

Ever been frustrated when trying to slice raw chicken or turkey into thin, neat pieces? Here's a nifty solution for you! Freeze the poultry for about one hour or until firm and partially frozen. Using a sharp knife, slice poultry across the grain to the desired thickness. You'll get perfectly thin slices every time!

Get the Facts on Food Safety

Food safety concerns everyone, from food manufacturers, food processors and packagers and supermarkets to everyday people who prepare and cook food in their homes. Why worry about food safety? Because microorganisms are always with us, on people and animals, in the air and water and on food—and especially on poultry.

Safe handling is particularly important to prevent the spread of salmonella, a very prevalent bacteria found in water and soil, and in the intestinal tract and on the skin of humans and all animals and birds. Because it is so common, salmonella may be present in raw foods, such as chicken and turkey, and may cause illness if the bird is improperly handled or undercooked. Someone infected with salmonella develops flu-like symptoms six to forty-eight hours after eating, and the illness can last two to seven days. It's also important to note that salmonella can be fatal under certain conditions, such as compromised immune systems, the very young and the very old.

Cutting up a Whole Chicken

You'll find it economical to purchase a whole chicken, then cut it into parts yourself. Don't worry; it's not difficult. Get the best results—safely—by using a sharp boning knife or poultry shears to cut chicken. Boning knives have a slim, pointed blade and a wide handle. Poultry shears, also known as curved shears, are made of stainless steel and are about 9 1/2 inches long with slightly curved blades and serrated edges. Unlike traditional scissors, poultry shears have a spring-loaded hinge design so they can exert the necessary force to cut chicken bones and cartilage. The lower blade usually has a notch near the hinge for the purpose of cutting through the smaller bones. After each use, wash with hot, soapy water and dry very thoroughly with paper towels, so they won't rust.

1. Place chicken, breast up, on cutting board. Remove wing from body by cutting into wing joint with a sharp knife, rolling knife to let the blade follow through at the curve of the joint as shown. Repeat with remaining wing.

2. Cut off each leg by cutting skin between the thigh and body of the chicken; continue cutting through the meat between the tail and hip joint, cutting as closely as possible to the backbone. Bend leg back until hip joint pops out as shown.

3. Continue cutting around bone and pulling leg from body until meat is separated from the bone as shown. Cut through remaining skin. Repeat on other side.

4. Separate thigh and drumstick by cutting about 1/8 inch from the fat line toward the drumstick side as shown. (A thin white fat line runs crosswise at joint between drumstick and thigh.) Repeat with remaining leg.

5. Separate back from breast by holding body, neck end down, and cutting downward along each side of backbone through the rib joints.

6. Bend breast halves back to pop out the keel bone; remove keel bone (for more detail, see step 2 on page 12). Using poultry shears or knife, cut breast into halves through wishbone; cut each breast half into halves.

How to Bone a Chicken Breast

Chicken breasts are available both whole and split in half. If you're starting with a split breast, jump right to step 3 in the directions below. For best results, use a boning knife with a 6-inch blade.

1. Bend breast halves back to pop out the keel bone; remove keel bone.

2. Loosen keel bone and white cartilage by running the tip of the index finger around both sides. Pull out bone in one or two pieces.

3. Working with one side of the breast, insert tip of knife under long rib bone. Resting knife against bones, use steady and even pressure to gradually trim meat away from bones. Cut rib cage away from breast, cutting through shoulder joint to remove entire rib cage. Repeat on other side.

4. Turn chicken breast over and cut away wishbone. Slip knife under white tendons on either side of breast; loosen and pull out tendons (grasp end of tendons with paper towel if tendons are slippery). Remove skin if desired. Cut breasts into halves; cut each breast half into halves if desired.

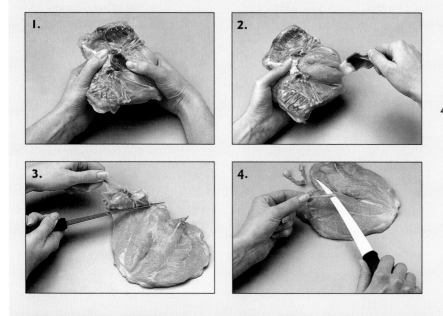

The Real Scoop about Bacteria, Food Spoilage and Food Poisoning

MYTH

Roasting poultry in a brown paper bag makes it more moist.

FACT

Use oven-roasting bags designed to be used in the oven instead (they are available in your grocery store in the same section as foil and plastic wrap). Paper bags are not sanitary and may catch on fire. Many brown paper bag recipes also state to turn the oven off for a certain period of time and then turn the heat back on. This may cause the temperature to fall too low, allowing illness-causing bacteria to grow. Properly cooked chicken can be moist and tender—without the brown paper bag.

MYTH

I can cook poultry in my dishwasher.

FACT

Of course we all know dishwashers weren't designed to cook foods, but dishwasher-cooking recipes have circulated like urban legends. A dishwasher cannot reach or sustain a high enough temperature to cook poultry. This is one urban legend to pass by.

MYTH

I can cut up raw poultry on a wooden cutting board.

FACT

Wooden cutting boards should not be used for cutting up or preparing raw poultry, meat or fish. The porous surface of wood and any cracks in the board can capture bacteria and allow it to grow. They are also harder to clean thoroughly. Use only plastic cutting boards for cutting up raw poultry, meat or fish; after cutting, clean the cutting board thoroughly by washing with a mixture of 2 teaspoons of chlorine bleach to 1 quart (4 cups) water.

MYTH

If food doesn't smell bad or look bad, it's okay to eat.

FACT

Bacteria that cause food to spoil can grow at refrigerator temperatures. Food spoilage can make food smell bad, and various molds can form on the food, which is an obvious clue to throw it out! *However, several common bacteria can spoil food without leaving any telltale signs of odor or appearance.*

When in doubt, throw it out! Eating questionable food and getting sick isn't worth any of the money that would be saved.

MYTH

"We've always left turkey leftovers out on the counter after dinner to cool and then to make sandwiches with them later on. Nobody has ever gotten sick, so why should I change the way I do things?"

FACT

To help prevent the growth of illness-causing bacteria, never leave foods out longer than two hours. Most food-poisoning bacteria don't grow at refrigerator temperatures (although some do), but they thrive at room temperatures (60° to 90°). These bacteria (such as *Salmonella, Staphylococcus, Listeria, Clostridium perfringens* and *Clostridium botulinum*) are also called *pathogens*. Eating these types of bacteria may lead to sickness, disease or even death. *Unfortunately, appearance, taste or smell do not always reveal these bacteria.*

Handling Food Safely

The Basics

- A standard rule, recommended by the U.S. Department of Agriculture, is to keep hot foods hot (above 140°) and cold foods cold (below 40°). Cooking and refrigeration can control most food-poisoning bacteria.

- Keep everything in the kitchen very clean because most bacteria get into food through improper handling. Keep countertops, appliances, utensils and dishes sanitary by cleaning with hot, soapy water or other cleaners.

- Don't allow hot or cold foods to remain at room temperature for more than two hours, including preparation time. Bacteria thrive in room-temperature and lukewarm food.

- Once food has been cooked, keep it hot until serving time, or refrigerate it as soon as possible. Immediately place hot food in the refrigerator unless doing so will raise the refrigerator temperature to above 45°. Food will cool more quickly in shallow containers (less than 2 inches deep) because it is spread out in a thinner layer.

- Wash hands thoroughly with hot, soapy water. If you have any kind of cut on your skin or infection on your hands, avoid handling food, or wear protective plastic gloves.

- Use disposable paper towels when working with or cleaning up after preparing raw poultry, meat, fish or seafood. If using dishcloths, wash them in the washing machine with hot or warm water and detergent before using them again.

Handling Raw Poultry

- For specific information on storing poultry, go to the Poultry Storage information on page 9. You will find a lot of good information to help you.

- Remove giblets (gizzard, heart and neck) if present, and rinse the cavity of the bird. Rub the cavity lightly with salt, if you like; however, do not salt the cavity if the bird will be stuffed.

- Wash your hands in hot, soapy water before and after handling raw poultry.

- Do not use wooden cutting boards for raw poultry. Hard-plastic cutting boards are less porous and therefore safer, and are easily cleaned or washed in a dishwasher. After working with raw poultry, wash the plastic boards with a mixture of 2 teaspoons chlorine bleach to 1 quart (4 cups) of water. Wash any knives used in hot, soapy water.

- Use disposable paper towels when working with or cleaning up after preparing raw poultry. If using dishcloths, wash them in your washing machine with hot or warm water and detergent before using them again, so they won't contaminate the surfaces they touch with harmful bacteria. Throw away dirty or mildewed dish sponges.

- Be careful not to transfer potential bacteria from raw meat to cooked meat. For example, never carry raw poultry to the grill on a platter and then serve cooked poultry on the same unwashed platter. Do not cut up raw poultry and then use the same knife and cutting board to prepare other foods unless both have been washed thoroughly.

Stuffing Poultry

- Don't pack the stuffing tightly into the cavity of the bird. Always stuff the poultry cavity loosely, so the stuffing cooks all the way through. The center of the stuffing must reach 165°. Never store leftover stuffing inside poultry because it can't cool quickly enough. Always remove the cooked stuffing from the cavity and store it in a separate container.

- Never stuff a chicken or turkey and then refrigerate or freeze it for later roasting; always stuff it just before cooking. This will help prevent any bacteria from contaminating the stuffing.

Stuffing Alternatives

You don't need to fill poultry with stuffing. Some people just add a couple of quartered onions and a clove or two of garlic to the cavity; others add wedges of fresh lemon or orange and fresh herbs—it's up to you. It's just fine to bake stuffing in a covered casserole dish alongside the poultry. In fact, many people love it this way because during the last 30 minutes or so of baking they can remove the cover from the stuffing so the top of the stuffing gets nicely crisp, crunchy and golden brown.

Cooking Poultry

Always cook chicken and turkey until well done, never medium or rare. Don't stop cooking poultry partway through and then finish cooking it again later, because partial cooking may encourage bacteria growth before cooking is complete. The U.S. Department of Agriculture recommends using a meat thermometer when cooking whole chicken or turkey. When using a meat thermometer, the internal temperature should reach:

180° for whole birds

170° for whole turkey breasts, bone-in pieces, boneless pieces

165° for stuffing

Check It Out!

Call the U.S. Department of Agriculture's Meat and Poultry Hotline for answers to your poultry questions. The toll-free number is 1-800-535-4555. Calls are taken from 10:00 A.M. to 4 P.M. eastern time Monday through Friday.

For free information on Food Safety, write to Publications, Room 1165-S, USDA, Washington, DC 20250.

Betty Crocker would love to hear from you! You can contact her in one of the following ways:
Call: 1-800-437-3480
Web Site: **www.bettycrocker.com**

Thermometer Facts
Types of Thermometers

Several types of meat thermometers are available. It's important to choose the right one for the job!

- A **meat thermometer** (also called a meat and poultry thermometer or roast-yeast thermometer) is designed to be inserted and left in poultry or meat during cooking. The temperature gauge of this type of thermometer is protected by stainless steel, making it safe for use in the oven. This thermometer generally has both a temperature gauge and markings indicating doneness for various types of meat and poultry. We recommend looking at the temperature gauge to determine doneness.

- An **instant-read thermometer** (also called instant or rapid response thermometer) is designed to take an almost immediate temperature reading of the food being cooked (within one minute of insertion). This type of thermometer *cannot be left in the oven*. This thermometer has only a temperature gauge under a plastic cover; if left in the oven, this cover will melt and could damage the gauge, resulting in inaccurate temperature readings.

Where Do I Put the Thermometer?

- **Whole Chicken or Turkey:** Insert meat thermometer so tip is in the thickest part of the inside thigh muscle and does not touch bone.

- **Whole Turkey Breast:** Insert meat thermometer so tip is in the thickest part of the breast muscle and does not touch bone.

- **Boneless Turkey Breast:** Insert meat thermometer so tip is in center of the thickest part of breast muscle.

Checking for Doneness without a Thermometer

Poultry doneness can be checked without a meat thermometer by using a sharp knife or fork. Here's how to tell when poultry is done:

- **Whole Chicken and Turkey:** Juice is no longer pink when center of thigh is cut and drumstick (leg) moves easily when lifted or twisted.

- **Whole Turkey Breast:** Juice is no longer pink when center is cut.

- **Cut-up Broiler-Fryers or Bone-in Pieces:** Juice is no longer pink when centers of thickest pieces are cut.

- **Boneless Pieces:** Juice is no longer pink when centers of thickest pieces are cut.

- **Small Pieces (for stir-fry, fajitas or chicken tenders):** Centers are no longer pink.

- **Ground Chicken and Turkey:** Meat is no longer pink.

- **Poultry Cooked in a Sauce or with Other Ingredients:** When checking for doneness, be sure you are checking that the *juice of the poultry* is no longer pink, not any other liquids being cooked with the poultry.

All of our recipes include directions on how to tell when the dish is properly cooked, which may include time, temperature, appearance or any combination of these.

Roasting Chicken and Turkey

Remove giblets (gizzard, heart and neck) if present, and rinse the cavity of the bird. Rub the cavity lightly with salt, if you like; however, do not salt the cavity if the bird will be stuffed. If you will be stuffing the bird, stuff just before roasting to prevent any bacteria in the raw poultry from contaminating the stuffing. You'll need about 3/4 cup stuffing per pound of poultry. Fill the wishbone area with stuffing first. For turkey, fasten the neck skin to the back with a skewer (this is not necessary for chicken). Fold the wings across the back with the tips touching. Fill the cavity lightly; don't pack it in, because the stuffing will expand during roasting. For chicken, tie or skewer the drumsticks (legs) to the tail. For turkey, tuck drumsticks (legs) under the band of skin at the tail, or tie or skewer to the tail.

Place the bird, breast side up, on a rack in a shallow roasting pan. Brush it with melted margarine or butter. Do not add water. Do not cover. Insert an ovenproof meat thermometer (not the instant-read type, which is not ovenproof), so the tip is in the thickest part of the inside thigh muscle and does not touch bone. Use the table below for approximate roasting times, but use the temperature as the final doneness guide. For turkey, place a tent of aluminum foil loosely over turkey when it begins to turn golden. When two-thirds done, cut band or remove tie or skewer holding legs.

Timetable for Roasting Chicken and Turkey

Poultry Type (whole)	Uncooked Weight (pounds)	Temperature	Approximate Oven Roasting Time (hours)*
Chicken (not stuffed)	3 to 3 1/2	375°	1 3/4 to 2
Chicken (stuffed)	3 to 3 1/2	325°	2 to 2 1/2
Turkey (not stuffed)	8 to 12	325°	2 3/4 to 3
	12 to 14	325°	3 to 3 3/4
	14 to 18	325°	3 3/4 to 4 1/4
	18 to 20	325°	4 1/4 to 4 1/2
	20 to 24	325°	4 1/2 to 5
Turkey (stuffed)	8 to 12	325°	3 to 3 1/2
	12 to 14	325°	3 1/2 to 4
	14 to 18	325°	4 to 4 1/2
	18 to 20	325°	4 1/4 to 4 3/4
	20 to 24	325°	4 3/4 to 5 1/4

*Types of ovens, actual oven temperatures and shape and tenderness of the bird will affect roasting times. Begin checking turkey doneness about 1 hour before end of recommended roasting time. For prestuffed store-bought turkeys, follow package directions carefully; do not use this timetable.

Roast the bird until the thermometer temperature reaches 180° and the juice is no longer pink when the center of a thigh is cut. The drumsticks (legs) should move easily when lifted and twisted. If the bird is stuffed, the center of the stuffing must reach an internal temperature of 165°; the same is true for prestuffed store-bought poultry. When done, remove the bird from the oven and let it stand about 15 minutes for easiest carving. This resting period allows the meat to become firmer, making it easier to carve smooth, uniform slices.

Great Grilling

Who can resist the aroma of food sizzling on a hot grill? Food cooked over an open flame just always seems to taste better! Check out our grilling chapter, starting on page 174, for recipes that are sure to tempt your taste-buds and get you inspired to fire up the coals. Grilling is easy, if you know the secrets to perfect grilling. Here's the scoop to get you started.

Lighting the Coals

- Light the coals at least 30 minutes before beginning to grill. Coals usually take between 30 and 45 minutes to reach the proper cooking temperature.

- When are the coals ready? In the daylight, the coals should be 80 percent ashy gray. After dark, the coals should have an even red glow. Bright red coals are too hot, black coals are too cool and a mix of red and black coals gives off uneven heat. Grilling over coals that are too cool can cause the food to have an off flavor from charcoal lighter that has not vaporized.

Grilling Poultry

Poultry Type	Weight (Pounds)	Grilling Method	Temperature	Cooking Time and Doneness
Whole chicken	3 to 3 1/2	Indirect	Medium	1 to 1 1/2 hours or until meat thermometer reads 180° and juice is no longer pink when center of thigh is cut.
Whole turkey	8 to 10	Indirect	Medium	3 to 4 hours or until meat thermometer reads 180° and juice is no longer pink when center of thigh is cut.
Whole turkey breast	3 1/2 to 4	Indirect	Medium	1 to 1 1/4 hours or until meat thermometer reads 170° and juice is no longer pink when center is cut.
Cornish game hen (split birds in half before grilling for best results)	3	Direct	Medium	30 to 40 minutes or until meat thermometer reads 180° and juice pink when center of thigh is cut.
Broiler-fryer, cut-up	2 to 2 1/2	Direct	Medium	35 to 40 minutes or until juice is no longer pink when centers of thickest pieces are cut.*
Chicken breasts (with bone)	1	Direct	Medium	20 to 25 minutes or until juice is no longer pink when centers of thickest pieces are cut.
Chicken breasts (boneless and not flattened)	1 1/4	Direct	Medium	15 to 20 minutes or until juice is no longer pink when centers of thickest pieces are cut.
Chicken breasts (boneless and flattened to 1/4-inch thickness)	1 1/4	Direct	Medium	10 to 15 minutes or until no longer pink in center
Chicken wings	2 to 2 1/2	Direct	Medium	12 to 18 minutes or until juice is no longer pink when centers of thickest pieces are cut.
Ground chicken or turkey patties	1 (1/2-inch-thick patties)	Direct	Medium	15 to 20 minutes or until no longer pink in center.
Turkey breast tenderloins	1 to 1 1/2	Direct	Medium	20 to 30 minutes or until juice is no longer pink when centers of thickest pieces are cut.
Turkey breast slices	1 to 1 1/2	Direct	Medium	8 to 10 minutes or until no longer pink in center.

* Dark meat may take longer to cook.

Carving Poultry

When carving poultry, get the best results—safely—by using a sharp knife and a meat fork. A carving knife works the best because it has a long, curved blade. A meat fork has a long handle and two tines. Carve poultry on a stable cutting surface, such a cutting board. Carving is simpler if the bird is allowed to stand for 15 to 20 minutes before cutting. This resting period allows the meat to become firmer and the juices to stay in the bird, making it easier to carve smooth, uniform slices.

How to Carve Chicken and Turkey

1. Place bird, breast up, with legs to carver's right if right-handed and to the left if left-handed. Remove ties or skewers.

2. While gently pulling leg and thigh away from body, cut through joint between leg and body. Separate drumstick (leg) and thigh by cutting down through connecting joint.

- **Special Note for Turkey:** Remove and separate drumstick (leg) and thigh as directed above, and serve them whole or carve them. To carve, remove meat from drumstick (leg) by slicing at an angle, and slice thigh by cutting even slices parallel to the bone.

3. Make a deep horizontal cut into breast just above wing. Insert fork in top of breast, and starting halfway up breast, carve thin slices down to the horizontal cut, working from outer edge of bird to the center.

4. Now just repeat steps 1 through 3 on the other side of the bird!

DIRECT HEAT: Grilling method where poultry is cooked on the grill rack directly over the heat source. This method is used in all grilling recipes in this book except for whole chicken, whole turkey and whole turkey breast.

INDIRECT METHOD: Grilling method where poultry is cooked away from the heat. It's the method to choose for longer-cooking poultry, such as whole birds and whole turkey breasts. If using coals, arrange hot coals around the edge of the firebox, and place a drip pan under the grilling area. If using a dual-burner gas grill, heat only one side, and place food over the burner that is not lit. For single-burner gas grills, place food in a foil tray or on several layers of aluminum foil and use low heat (grilling times may be longer than chart indicates).

Readying the Grill Rack

- Grease or oil the rack before lighting the coals or turning on the gas.

- Place the grill rack 4 to 6 inches above the coals or gas burners.

Great Grilling Tips

- Cook poultry pieces evenly by placing the meatier pieces in the center of the grill rack and smaller pieces around the edges. Turn the pieces frequently.

- Keep poultry moist and juicy by turning pieces with tongs instead of piercing them with a fork.

- Prevent poultry from overbrowning or burning (and avoid calls to the fire department!) by brushing sauces on during the last 15 to 20 minutes of grilling, especially when using sauces that contain tomato or sugar because they can burn easily or cause flare-ups.

Grilling Food Safely

- Never place cooked poultry on the same unwashed platter that raw poultry has been on.

- Before serving leftover marinades and sauces that have touched raw poultry, heat them to a rolling boil and boil 1 minute.

Poaching Chicken

Poached chicken is great to use recipes calling for cooked chicken. Check out the many different ways to add flavor to the poached chicken, too. It's so easy; here's how:

1. Put chicken pieces, either bone-in or boneless, in a saucepan or skillet that is large enough so that the chicken can be completely covered with liquid (see suggestions in list below). Add enough liquid just to cover chicken.

2. To increase flavor, add herbs, seasonings and vegetables to the liquid, and heat until boiling. Reduce the heat to low. Cover and simmer the chicken until the juice is no longer pink when the centers of the thickest pieces are cut. Allow about 15 minutes per pound for it to be completely cooked.

3. Refrigerate chicken in poaching liquid until cool. Remove chicken from liquid and cut up as desired.

Cooking Liquid Ideas
- Chicken broth
- Fruit juices (apple, orange or pineapple)
- Water (with chicken bouillon cubes or granules added)
- Wine (white or red wine will both give great flavor, but red wine will discolor the chicken)
- Combinations of any of the above

Other Flavor Makers
- Celery (1 rib cut into small pieces or chopped)
- Chilies (1 or 2 small chilies left whole or chopped)
- Citrus peel (orange, lemon or lime)
- Garlic cloves (1 or 2 cloves left whole, halved or finely chopped)
- Gingerroot (1 slice about the size of a quarter or 1 teaspoon grated or finely chopped)
- Herbs, fresh or dried (4 to 5 sprigs or 1 tablespoon chopped)

- Onions (1 medium onion halved, quartered or chopped)
- Peppercorns (1 teaspoon)
- Seasonings (about 1 teaspoon dried herb leaves such as basil or oregano or 1/2 teaspoon of seasoning such as cumin, chili powder, garlic powder or onion powder)
- Vegetables, small whole (4 or 5 baby-cut carrots, or small onions)

How Much Poultry?

Cubed, Chopped or Shredded Chicken or Turkey

When a recipe calls for cubed, chopped or shredded cooked chicken, how much should you cook? Here are some guidelines to follow.

START WITH	TO EQUAL
2 1/2 to 3 pounds broiler-fryer chicken	2 1/2 to 3 cups
1 1/2 pounds whole bone-in chicken breast	2 cups
1 1/2 pounds boneless, skinless chicken breast or turkey tenderloins	3 cups
1 1/2 pounds chicken thighs or drumsticks (legs)	1 3/4 cups
1 1/2 pounds whole turkey breast	2 1/2 cups
6 to 8 pounds turkey	7 to 10 cups

Whole Chicken or Turkey or Cut-up Parts

As a general rule, when buying whole chicken or turkey or cut-up parts, plan on about 3/4 pound (including bone weight) per person. Then figure in enough for leftovers, too, if you like.

Microwaving Poultry

Arrange poultry pieces with skin sides up and thickest parts to outside edge in a microwavable dish that's large enough to hold the pieces in a single layer. Cover with plastic wrap, folding back one corner to vent. Microwave as directed below. Bone-in pieces are done when juice of chicken is no longer pink when centers of thickest pieces are cut; boneless pieces when chicken or turkey is no longer pink in the center; and ground chicken or turkey until no longer pink.

POULTRY TYPE	WEIGHT (POUNDS)	POWER LEVEL	COOKING TIME (MINUTES)
Chicken			
Broiler-fryer, cut-up	2 to 2 1/2	High	9 to 17, rotating dish half turn after 5.
Breast halves, bone in, with skin	about 1 1/4	High	8 to 10, rotating dish half turn after 4.
Breast halves, skinless, boneless	about 1 1/2	High	8 to 10, rotating dish half turn after 4.
Wings	2 to 2 1/2	High	12 to 15, rotating dish half turn after 6.
Legs or thighs	2	High	16 to 19, rotating dish half turn after 10.
Ground	1	High	4 to 7, stirring after 2.
Rock Cornish Hens			
One	1 to 1 1/2	High	7 to 10, turning over after 4, until thermometer reads 180°.
Two	2 to 3	High	13 to 18, turning over after 7, until thermometer reads 180°.
Turkey			
Boneless breast	3 to 4	Medium	40 to 55, turning half over after 20, until thermometer reads 170°.
Breast tenderloins	about 1 1/2	High	5 to 8, rotating dish half turn after 3.
Breast slices	1	High	3 to 5, rotating dish half turn after 2.
Ground	1	High	4 to 7, stirring after 2.

Use Your Favorites!

Are you partial to certain parts of the chicken, such as breasts or drumsticks? No problem! Use any of your favorite chicken pieces in any of the recipes in this book that call for a cut-up broiler-fryer chicken. Just substitute the same weight of breasts, thighs, drumsticks (legs) or wings for the cut-up broiler-fryer. If you choose to use all breasts or thighs, which are thicker and meatier than other pieces, you may need to increase the cooking time (check for doneness about every 5 minutes)—but it'll be worth the wait!

Nutrition Facts about Poultry

Type	Calories	Protein (g)	Fat (g)	Cholesterol (mg)
Chicken (3 ounces baked)				
Whole				
With skin	200	23	12	75
Without skin	162	25	6	75
Breast				
With skin	160	23	6	65
Without skin	145	26	4	70
Thigh				
With skin	215	22	13	75
Without skin	180	24	9	75
Drumstick				
With skin	180	24	9	75
Without skin	140	25	4	75
Wing				
With skin	245	23	17	75
Without skin	160	23	6	75
Ground	200	25	11	75
Turkey (3 ounces baked)				
Whole				
With skin	200	23	11.5	75
Without skin	160	25	6.5	75
Breast				
With skin	160	23	6.5	65
Without skin	120	26	1	70
Thigh				
With skin	180	24	9	70
Without skin	140	25	3.5	75
Drumstick				
With skin	180	24	9	70
Without skin	140	25	3.5	75
Wing				
With skin	195	23	10.5	75
Without skin	145	26	4	70
Ground	200	23	11.5	75

Moist Poultry Secrets

What is one of the biggest complaints cooks have about making chicken? It's too dry! Store-bought individually frozen or fresh chicken breasts have usually gone through a process in which the chicken was injected with a salt-water solution; these tend to be very tender, moist, juicy and are saltier. On the other hand, chicken breasts made without this process can be just a little less tender, moist and juicy. Whichever type you use, we offer you some great little secrets for moist and juicy chicken.

Secret #1

Wrap chicken tightly during storage to prevent it from drying out.

Secret #2

Marinating adds flavor and makes for juicy chicken. Marinate skinless boneless breasts for 1 to 2 hours and bone-in pieces up to 24 hours.

Secret #3

Brush chicken with milk, buttermilk, Dijon mustard or mayonnaise, then roll in bread crumbs, cracker crumbs or flour before cooking. The coating helps seal in moisture.

Secret #4

Cooking chicken with the skin on adds to the flavor, not the fat. Research has found that the fat does not transfer to the meat during cooking. So go ahead and leave the skin on—it helps keep the juices in, creates a moister, more tender meat and boosts the flavor. If you're watching your calories, fat and cholesterol, remove the skin after cooking and throw it away.

Secret #5

Don't overcook chicken or test too often for doneness. To test for doneness, use a knife to cut into the center of the thickest part of the chicken to see if the juice is no longer pink. Only test once or twice so the juices of the chicken stay in the chicken. Do not pierce the chicken with a thick, multi-tined fork or the chicken will lose an excessive amount of juice.

Secret #6

Don't undercook chicken either. Undercooked chicken will be tough and rubbery because it takes a certain amount of time and heat to soften the proteins in the chicken muscle.

Secret #7

Microwave chicken to partially cook it before grilling it. Not only does this save time, but it can also help prevent overcooked, burned chicken. To microwave, put the chicken, thickest parts to the outside edges, in a microwavable dish large enough to hold all the pieces in a single layer. Cover with plastic wrap, folding back one corner to allow steam to escape. Microwave on High for about 4 minutes per pound, rotating dish after half the cooking time, until edges begin to cook; drain. Immediately put chicken on the heated grill and grill according to recipe.

Secret #8

Use tongs instead of a fork to turn chicken pieces in the skillet or on the grill. A fork will pierce the meat and let the juices escape.

Wake up Your Taste Buds!

Wake up your tired taste buds! There is a world of tastes to explore and savor, from simple to fancy, mild to bold, familiar to exotic. So move over salt and pepper, because a flavor explosion is moving in on your territory. Whether your chicken is bathed in marinade or slathered with an intense rub, it's going to be good. With so many possibilities to consider, it was difficult to choose, but we picked some of our favorites for you. Give them a try—they are delicious and easy.

1. Start with 4 boneless, skinless chicken breast halves.
2. Flatten chicken breasts to 1/4-inch thick between plastic wrap or waxed paper (see also page 10).
3. Follow directions below.

Spicy Wine *Marinade*

ABOUT 3/4 CUP

1/2 cup olive or vegetable oil

1/4 cup white wine

1 teaspoon dried thyme leaves

1/2 teaspoon ground red pepper (cayenne)

1 clove garlic, finely chopped

1 teaspoon olive or vegetable oil

Mix all ingredients except 1 teaspoon oil. Combine chicken and marinade in a sealable plastic bag or shallow glass or plastic container. Seal bag or cover container and refrigerate at least 4 hours, but no longer than 24 hours.

Remove chicken from marinade. Heat 1 teaspoon oil in 12-inch nonstick skillet over medium heat. Cook chicken in oil 8 to 10 minutes, turning once, until chicken is no longer pink in center.

Santa Fe *Rub*

ABOUT 3 TABLESPOONS

1 tablespoon chili powder

1 tablespoon vegetable oil

1 teaspoon ground cumin

1/4 teaspoon salt

1/4 teaspoon ground chipotle chilies or red pepper (cayenne)

1 large clove garlic, finely chopped

2 tablespoons vegetable oil

Mix all ingredients except 2 tablespoons oil. Rub both sides of chicken with rub. Heat remaining oil in 12-inch nonstick skillet over medium heat. Cook chicken in oil 8 to 10 minutes, turning once, until chicken is no longer pink in center.

Sesame *Marinade*

ABOUT 1/2 CUP

1/4 cup seasoned rice wine vinegar

2 tablespoons vegetable oil

2 tablespoons sesame oil

1/2 teaspoon sugar

1 teaspoon vegetable oil

1 tablespoon sesame seed, toasted if desired

Mix all ingredients except 1 teaspoon vegetable oil and the sesame seed. Combine chicken and marinade in a sealable plastic bag or shallow glass or plastic container. Seal bag or cover container and refrigerate at least 4 hours, but no longer than 24 hours.

Remove chicken from marinade. Heat 1 teaspoon oil in 12-inch nonstick skillet over medium heat. Cook chicken in oil 8 to 10 minutes, turning once, until chicken is no longer pink in center. Spinkle with sesame seeds.

Cajun Spice *Rub*

ABOUT 1 TABLESPOON

1 teaspoon black pepper

1/2 teaspoon ground red pepper (cayenne)

1/2 teaspoon white pepper

1/2 teaspoon ground cumin

1/2 teaspoon ground nutmeg

1/2 teaspoon salt

2 tablespoons vegetable oil

Mix all ingredients except oil. Brush both sides of chicken with 1 tablespoon of the oil; rub with spice rub.

Heat remaining 1 tablespoon oil in 12-inch non-stick skillet over medium heat. Cook chicken in oil 8 to 10 minutes, turning once, until chicken is no longer pink in center.

Oriental Spice *Rub*

ABOUT 2 TABLESPOONS

1 tablespoon ground coriander

1 tablespoon five-spice powder

1 1/2 teaspoons packed brown sugar

1/2 teaspoon garlic powder

1/8 teaspoon pepper

2 tablespoons vegetable oil

Mix all ingredients except oil. Brush both sides of chicken with 1 tablespoon of the oil; rub with spice rub.

Heat remaining 1 tablespoon oil in 12-inch non-stick skillet over medium heat. Cook chicken in oil 8 to 10 minutes, turning once, until chicken is no longer pink in center.

Teriyaki *Marinade*

ABOUT 1/2 CUP

1/4 cup maple-flavored syrup

1/4 cup soy sauce

1 tablespoon vegetable oil

1 teaspoons ground ginger

2 cloves garlic, finely chopped

1 teaspoon vegetable oil

Mix all ingredients except 1 teaspoon oil. Combine chicken and marinade in a sealable plastic bag or shallow glass or plastic container. Seal bag or cover container and refrigerate at least 4 hours, but no longer than 24 hours.

Remove chicken from marinade. Heat oil in 12-inch nonstick skillet over medium heat. Cook chicken in oil 8 to 10 minutes, turning once, until chicken is no longer pink in center.

Indonesian *Marinade*

ABOUT 1 CUP

1 can (14 ounces) coconut milk (not cream of coconut)

1 tablespoon cider vinegar

1 teaspoon soy sauce

1 tablespoon curry powder

2 teaspoons sugar

1 teaspoon salt

1/2 teaspoon ground red pepper (cayenne)

1 teaspoon vegetable oil

Mix all ingredients except oil. Combine chicken and marinade in a sealable plastic bag or shallow glass or plastic container. Seal bag or cover container and refrigerate at least 4 hours, but no longer than 24 hours.

Remove chicken from marinade. Heat oil in 12-inch nonstick skillet over medium heat. Cook chicken in oil 8 to 10 minutes, turning once, until chicken is no longer pink in center.

Herb *Rub*

ABOUT 2 TABLESPOONS

1 tablespoon vegetable oil

1 tablespoon dried tarragon leaves

2 teaspoons dried thyme leaves

1 1/2 teaspoons dried sage leaves, crumbled

1/2 teaspoon onion powder

1/4 teaspoon salt

Mix all ingredients.

Maple-Bourbon *Marinade*

ABOUT 1/2 CUP

1/4 cup maple-flavored syrup

1/4 cup bourbon or apple juice

1/2 teaspoon salt

1 tablespoon vegetable oil

Mix all ingredients except oil. Combine chicken and marinade in a sealable plastic bag or shallow glass or plastic container. Seal bag or cover container and refrigerate at least 4 hours, but no longer than 24 hours.

Remove chicken from marinade. Heat oil in 12-inch nonstick skillet over medium heat. Cook chicken in oil 8 to 10 minutes, turning once, until chicken is no longer pink in center.

Lemon-Basil *Marinade*

ABOUT 1/2 CUP

1/4 cup vegetable oil

3 tablespoons lemon juice

1/4 cup chopped fresh or 1 teaspoon dried basil leaves

1/2 teaspoon lemon pepper seasoning

1 teaspoon vegetable oil

Mix all ingredients except 1 teaspoon oil. Combine chicken and marinade in a sealable plastic bag or shallow glass or plastic container. Seal bag or cover container and refrigerate at least 4 hours, but no longer than 24 hours.

Remove chicken from marinade. Heat 1 teaspoon oil in 12-inch nonstick skillet over medium heat. Cook chicken in oil 8 to 10 minutes, turning once, until chicken is no longer pink in center.

Chapter 1

Super Express. . .
30 Minutes or Less

Easy Pasta
and Sausage

PREP: 12 MIN ▪ COOK: 14 MIN ▪ 4 SERVINGS

3 cups uncooked radiatore (nugget) pasta (9 ounces)

4 turkey Italian sausages, cut into 2-inch pieces

1 large green bell pepper, cut into thin strips

1 cup marinara or spaghetti sauce

Shredded Parmesan cheese, if desired

Cook and drain pasta as directed on package. Cook sausages in 12-inch skillet over medium heat about 10 minutes, turning occasionally, until no longer pink; drain.

Stir bell pepper into sausages; cook 2 minutes. Stir in marinara sauce and pasta. Cook about 2 minutes or until hot. Sprinkle with cheese.

1 Serving: Calories 390 (Calories from Fat 90); Fat 10g (Saturated 3g); Cholesterol 35mg; Sodium 690mg; Carbohydrate 60g (Dietary Fiber 4g); Protein 19g
*% **Daily Value:** Vitamin A 10%; Vitamin C 38%; Calcium 4%; Iron 18%*
***Diet Exchanges:** 4 Starch, 1 Lean Meat, 1 Fat*

Betty's Tip

Turkey Italian sausages are available in two varieties, sweet and hot. Sweet sausages tend to have a stronger fennel flavor (reminiscent of licorice), and the hot sausages are spicier from the red peppers.

Pesto Chicken
and Pasta

PREP: 5 MIN ▪ COOK: 12 MIN ▪ 4 SERVINGS

3 cups uncooked farfalle (bow-tie) pasta (6 ounces)

2 cups cubed cooked chicken or turkey breast

1/2 cup pesto

1/2 cup coarsely chopped drained roasted red bell peppers (from 7-ounce jar)

Sliced ripe olives, if desired

Cook and drain pasta as directed on package, using 3-quart saucepan. Mix hot cooked pasta, chicken, pesto and bell peppers in same saucepan. Heat over low heat, stirring constantly, until hot. Garnish with olives.

1 Serving: Calories 565 (Calories from Fat 160); Fat 18g (Saturated 4g); Cholesterol 60mg; Sodium 290mg; Carbohydrate 71g (Dietary Fiber 4g); Protein 35g
% Daily Value: Vitamin A 8%; Vitamin C 24%; Calcium 12%; Iron 28%
Diet Exchanges: 3 Starch, 3 Lean Meat, 2 Vegetable, 2 Fat

Betty's Tip

Look for reduced-fat pesto
if you would like to shave
some fat grams from this
recipe. Another way to
cut back on the fat in
pesto is to skim off some
of the oil that rises to the
top of regular pesto.

Garden Chicken
and Fettuccine

PREP: 12 MIN ▪ COOK: 4 MIN ▪ 6 SERVINGS

8 ounces uncooked fettuccine

3 cups chopped cooked chicken

3 tablespoons olive or vegetable oil

1 teaspoon garlic salt

2 large tomatoes, chopped (2 cups)

Chopped fresh basil leaves, if desired

Cook and drain pasta as directed on package. Toss pasta and remaining ingredients except basil. Top with basil.

1 Serving: Calories 315 (Calories from Fat 115); Fat 13g (Saturated 3g); Cholesterol 90mg; Sodium 230mg; Carbohydrate 27g (Dietary Fiber 2g); Protein 25g
% Daily Value: Vitamin A 4%; Vitamin C 20%; Calcium 2%; Iron 14%
Diet Exchanges: 1 Starch, 2 1/2 Medium-Fat Meat, 2 Vegetable

Try This

Add more color to this tasty pasta dish by using tomato-basil, spinach or herb pasta.

Vegetable-Chicken
Stir-Fry

PREP: 5 MIN ▪ COOK: 7 MIN ▪ 4 SERVINGS

2 tablespoons vegetable oil

1 pound boneless, skinless chicken breast halves or thighs, cut into 1-inch pieces

3 cups cut-up assorted vegetables (bell peppers, broccoli flowerets, shredded carrots)

1 clove garlic, finely chopped

1/2 cup stir-fry sauce

Heat 1 tablespoon of the oil in 12-inch skillet or wok over high heat. Add chicken; stir-fry about 3 minutes or until no longer pink in center. Remove from skillet.

Heat remaining 1 tablespoon oil in skillet. Add vegetables and garlic; stir-fry about 2 minutes or until vegetables are crisp-tender. Add chicken and stir-fry sauce. Cook and stir about 2 minutes or until hot.

1 Serving: Calories 235 (Calories from Fat 100); Fat 11g (Saturated 2g); Cholesterol 70mg; Sodium 1900mg; Carbohydrate 9g (Dietary Fiber 3g); Protein 28g
*% **Daily Value:** Vitamin A 66%; Vitamin C 78%; Calcium 4%; Iron 10%*
Diet Exchanges: 3 1/2 Lean Meat, 2 Vegetable

Betty's Tip

Add toasty crunch with toasted wonton wrappers! You'll find wonton wrappers in the produce or freezer section of most grocery stores. Cut wonton wrappers into thin strips, and bake on ungreased cookie sheet at 350° for 5 to 7 minutes or until light golden brown. Top each serving with whole or broken toasted wonton strips.

Szechuan Chicken and Pasta

PREP: 5 MIN ▪ COOK: 25 MIN ▪ 4 SERVINGS

1 pound boneless, skinless chicken breast halves, cut into 3/4- to 1-inch pieces

1 medium onion, cut into thin wedges

2 cups water

1 1/2 cups uncooked fusilli pasta (3 ounces)

1 package (1 pound 5 ounces) frozen Szechuan stir-fry mix with vegetables, Szechuan sauce and peanuts

Spray 12-inch nonstick skillet with cooking spray; heat over medium-high heat. Add chicken and onion; stir-fry 3 to 5 minutes or until chicken is light brown.

Stir in water; heat to boiling. Stir in pasta. Cook 8 to 10 minutes, stirring occasionally, until pasta is almost tender (do not drain).

Stir in packet of sauce mix from stir-fry mix until well blended. Stir in vegetables. Reduce heat to medium. Cover and cook 8 to 9 minutes, stirring occasionally, until vegetables are crisp-tender. Sprinkle with peanuts from stir-fry mix.

1 Serving: Calories 380 (Calories from Fat 90); Fat 10g (Saturated 2g); Cholesterol 50mg; Sodium 620mg; Carbohydrate 49g (Dietary Fiber 7g); Protein 30g
*% **Daily Value:** Vitamin A 18%; Vitamin C 38%; Calcium 8%; Iron 22%*
***Diet Exchanges:** 3 Starch, 2 Lean Meat, 1 Vegetable*

Betty's Tip

For an additional time-saver, look for thinly presliced chicken breast strips in the meat aisle (the package may be labeled "chicken for stir-fry"). You'll need about 1 pound of strips for this recipe.

Sweet-and-Sour Chicken

PREP: 5 MIN ▪ COOK 10 MIN ▪ 4 SERVINGS

1 package (10 ounces) frozen breaded fully cooked chicken chunks

1/4 cup water

1 bag (16 ounces) frozen broccoli, carrots and water chestnuts

1 can (20 ounces) pineapple chunks, drained

1 jar (9 ounces) sweet-and-sour sauce (1 1/4 cups)

Prepare chicken chunks as directed on package. While chicken is baking, heat water to boiling in 3-quart saucepan. Add frozen vegetables; reduce heat to medium. Cover and cook 5 to 6 minutes or until hot; drain. Return vegetables to saucepan.

Stir chicken, pineapple and sweet-and-sour sauce into vegetables in saucepan. Cook over medium heat 3 to 4 minutes, stirring occasionally, until hot.

1 Serving: Calories 415 (Calories from Fat 145); Fat 16g (Saturated 4g); Cholesterol 45mg; Sodium 780mg; Carbohydrate 55g (Dietary Fiber 5g); Protein 18g
% Daily Value: Vitamin A 40%; Vitamin C 42%; Calcium 8%; Iron 16%
Diet Exchanges: 2 Starch, 1 Lean Meat, 2 Vegetable, 1 Fruit, 2 Fat

Betty's Tip

This would taste great served over hot cooked rice and sprinkled with toasted sesame seed.

Mediterranean
Skillet Chicken

PREP: 5 MIN ■ COOK: 25 MIN ■ 4 SERVINGS

2 tablespoons olive or vegetable oil

4 boneless, skinless chicken breast halves (1 pound)

1 can (14 1/2 ounces) Italian-style stewed tomatoes, undrained

1/2 cup sliced ripe olives

1 teaspoon grated lemon peel

Heat oil in 12-inch nonstick skillet over medium-high heat. Cook chicken in oil 5 minutes, turning once, until brown.

Stir in remaining ingredients. Heat to boiling; reduce heat to low. Cover and simmer 15 to 20 minutes or until juice of chicken is no longer pink when centers of thickest pieces are cut.

1 Serving: Calories 260 (Calories from Fat 115); Fat 13g (Saturated 2g); Cholesterol 75mg; Sodium 500mg; Carbohydrate 9g (Dietary Fiber 1g); Protein 28g
% Daily Value: Vitamin A 6%; Vitamin C 10%; Calcium 4%; Iron 10%
Diet Exchanges: 4 Lean Meat, 2 Vegetable

Betty's Tip

There are many different olive oils available. Extra virgin olive oil comes from the first pressing of the olives and has a fruity flavor and deep golden to green color. Virgin olive oil is also from the first pressing of olives, but has a slightly more acidic flavor. Pure olive oil or olive oil is a combination of refined olive and virgin or extra virgin olive oil.

Blue Cheese
Tenders

PREP: 5 MIN ▪ COOK: 12 MIN ▪ 4 SERVINGS

I tablespoon vegetable oil

I pound chicken breast tenders

I tablespoon lemon juice

I clove garlic, finely chopped

1/3 cup blue cheese dressing

Hot cooked farfalle (bow-tie) pasta, if desired

Crumbled blue cheese, if desired

Heat oil in 10-inch skillet over medium-high heat. Cook chicken, lemon juice and garlic in oil 8 to 10 minutes, stirring occasionally, until chicken is no longer pink in center.

Stir in dressing. Cook 2 to 4 minutes, stirring frequently, until hot. Serve over farfalle. Sprinkle with blue cheese.

1 Serving: Calories 230 (Calories from Fat 110); Fat 12g (Saturated 2g); Cholesterol 70mg; Sodium 350mg; Carbohydrate 5g (Dietary Fiber 0g); Protein 26g
% Daily Value: Vitamin A 0%; Vitamin C 0%; Calcium 2%; Iron 4%
Diet Exchanges: 3 1/2 Lean Meat, 1 Vegetable, 1/2 Fat

Betty's Tip

The combination of toasted walnuts and blue cheese is a marriage made in heaven. To toast walnuts, place them in an uncovered shallow pan and toast in a 350° oven about 10 minutes, stirring occasionally, until golden brown.

One-Pan Potatoes
and Chicken

PREP: 10 MIN ▪ COOK: 20 MIN ▪ 4 SERVINGS

2 tablespoons vegetable oil

8 medium red potatoes, thinly sliced

1 pound boneless, skinless chicken breasts, cut into thin strips

1 medium red bell pepper, cut into thin strips

1 teaspoon garlic salt

Heat oil in 12-inch nonstick skillet over medium heat. Add potatoes, chicken and bell pepper to skillet. Sprinkle with garlic salt. Cook 15 to 20 minutes, stirring frequently, until chicken is no longer pink in center and potatoes are tender.

1 Serving: Calories 385 (Calories from Fat 100); Fat 11g (Saturated 2g); Cholesterol 75mg; Sodium 320mg; Carbohydrate 46g (Dietary Fiber 5g); Protein 31g
% Daily Value: Vitamin A 18%; Vitamin C 66%; Calcium 4%; Iron 18%
Diet Exchanges: 3 Starch, 3 Lean Meat

Try This

Let your imagination and your tastebuds run wild by trying different potatoes for color and flavor. Choose Yukon gold, purple, yellow Finnish or Texas finger potatoes.

Easy Mexican Chicken and Beans

PREP: 8 MIN ▪ COOK: 20 MIN ▪ 4 SERVINGS

1 pound cut-up boneless chicken breast for stir-fry

1 envelope (1 1/4 ounces) taco seasoning mix

1 can (15 to 16 ounces) black or pinto beans, rinsed and drained

1 can (11 ounces) whole kernel corn with red and green peppers, undrained

1/4 cup water

Flour tortillas, if desired

Spray 10-inch nonstick skillet with cooking spray. Cook chicken in skillet over medium-high heat 8 to 10 minutes, stirring occasionally, until no longer pink in center.

Stir in seasoning mix, beans, corn and water. Cook over medium-high heat 8 to 10 minutes, stirring frequently, until sauce is slightly thickened. Serve with tortillas.

1 Serving: Calories 335 (Calories from Fat 45); Fat 5g (Saturated 1g); Cholesterol 70mg; Sodium 780mg; Carbohydrate 48g (Dietary Fiber 12g); Protein 37g
% Daily Value: Vitamin A 10%; Vitamin C 10%; Calcium 8%; Iron 24%
Diet Exchanges: 2 Starch, 3 1/2 Very Lean Meat, 3 Vegetable

Betty's Tip

Make a weekday Mexican fiesta by serving this tasty dish topped with sour cream, salsa and green chilies. Olé! Chips and guacamole are always popular, too.

Oriental Turkey
Patties

PREP: 10 MIN ▪ COOK: 16 MIN ▪ 4 PATTIES

1 pound ground turkey

1/4 cup sweet-and-sour sauce

1 can (8 ounces) whole water chestnuts, drained and chopped

4 medium green onions, sliced (1/4 cup)

Hot cooked Japanese curly noodles, if desired

Sweet-and-sour sauce, if desired

Set oven control to broil. Mix turkey, 1/4 cup sweet-and-sour sauce, the water chestnuts and onions. Shape mixture into 4 patties, each about 1/2 inch thick. Place on rack in broiler pan.

Broil with tops about 3 inches from heat 12 to 16 minutes, turning once, until no longer pink in center. Serve with noodles and sweet-and-sour sauce.

1 Serving: Calories 205 (Calories from Fat 65); Fat 7g (Saturated 2g); Cholesterol 75mg; Sodium 140mg; Carbohydrate 11g (Dietary Fiber 1g); Protein 25g
*% **Daily Value:*** Vitamin A 2%; Vitamin C 4%; Calcium 2%; Iron 8%
Diet Exchanges: 3 Lean Meat, 2 Vegetable

Betty's Tip

Try ground turkey breast for a lower-fat version, as it is only white meat. Regular ground turkey contains dark meat and skin, making it higher in fat. Serve these delicious patties with pea pods and sliced carrots.

Philly Turkey
Panini

PREP: 6 MIN ▪ COOK: 5 MIN ▪ 4 SANDWICHES

8 slices rye or pumpernickel bread, 1/2 inch thick

2 tablespoons margarine or butter, softened

1/2 pound thinly sliced cooked deli turkey

4 slices (1 ounce each) mozzarella cheese

1 medium green bell pepper, cut into rings

Spread one side of each bread slice with margarine. Place 4 bread slices margarine sides down; top with turkey, cheese and bell pepper. Top with remaining bread slices, margarine sides up.

Cover and cook sandwiches in 12-inch skillet over medium heat 4 to 5 minutes, turning once, until bread is crisp and cheese is melted.

1 Serving: Calories 315 (Calories from Fat 125); Fat 14g (Saturated 5g); Cholesterol 40mg; Sodium 1240mg; Carbohydrate 29g (Dietary Fiber 4g); Protein 22g
% Daily Value: Vitamin A 14%; Vitamin C 22%; Calcium 26%; Iron 10%
Diet Exchanges: 2 Starch, 2 Lean Meat, 1 1/2 Fat

Try This

You have many choices when buying sliced deli turkey. Try a smoked, mesquite, peppercorn or honey variety for a different flavor.

Chicken-Pesto
Panini

PREP: 8 MIN ▪ COOK: 5 MIN ▪ 4 SANDWICHES

**8 slices Italian bread,
1/2 inch thick**

**2 tablespoons margarine
or butter, softened**

**1/2 pound thinly sliced
cooked deli chicken**

4 tablespoons basil pesto

**4 slices (1 ounce each)
mozzarella cheese**

**Spaghetti sauce, warmed,
if desired**

Spread one side of each bread slice with margarine. Place 4 bread slices margarine sides down; top with chicken, pesto and cheese. Top with remaining bread slices, margarine sides up.

Cover and cook sandwiches in 12-inch skillet over medium heat 4 to 5 minutes, turning once, until bread is crisp and cheese is melted. Serve with spaghetti sauce.

1 Serving: Calories 395 (Calories from Fat 225); Fat 25g (Saturated 7g); Cholesterol 40mg; Sodium 1290mg; Carbohydrate 24g (Dietary Fiber 1g); Protein 20g
% Daily Value: Vitamin A 14%; Vitamin C 0%; Calcium 30%; Iron 10%
Diet Exchanges: 1 1/2 Starch, 2 Lean Meat, 4 Fat

Try This

Instead of Italian bread, try onion or herb focaccia for a traditional sandwich. Start by slicing focaccia horizontally in half, spread cut sides of focaccia with margarine. Cut focaccia into 4 wedges. Layer chicken, pesto and cheese on bottom wedges and place on large cookie sheet. Add tops of wedges, cut sides up, on cookie sheet sheet. Broil 4 to 6 inches from heat for 3 minutes. Place tops of focaccia on top of chicken, pesto and cheese.

Chicken Salad
on Focaccia

PREP: 10 MIN ■ 4 SANDWICHES

3 cups chopped cooked chicken

3 medium stalks celery, finely chopped (1 1/2 cups)

1/2 cup mayonnaise or salad dressing

1 teaspoon garlic-and-herb seasoning

1 round focaccia bread (10 to 12 inches in diameter), cut horizontally in half

Mix chicken, celery, mayonnaise and seasoning. Spread mixture over bottom half of focaccia bread; top with remaining half. Cut into wedges.

1 Serving: Calories 730 (Calories from Fat 405); Fat 45g (Saturated 8g); Cholesterol 105mg; Sodium 1090mg; Carbohydrate 48g (Dietary Fiber 2g); Protein 35g
% Daily Value: Vitamin A 6%; Vitamin C 4%; Calcium 4%; Iron 26%
Diet Exchanges: 3 Starch, 4 Lean Meat, 6 Fat

Try This

If you can't find garlic-and-herb seasoning, mix together 1/2 teaspoon dried basil leaves, 1/4 teaspoon dried thyme leaves, 1/4 teaspoon garlic powder and 1/8 teaspoon pepper.

Hot Chicken
Sub

PREP: 30 MIN ▪ 6 SERVINGS

6 frozen breaded chicken breast patties

1 loaf (1 pound) French bread, cut horizontally in half

1/2 cup creamy Italian dressing

Lettuce

1 large tomato, thinly sliced

Prepare chicken as directed on package.

Spread cut sides of bread with dressing. Layer lettuce, hot chicken patties and tomato on bottom half of bread. Top with top half of bread. Cut into slices.

1 Serving: Calories 525 (Calories from Fat 235); Fat 26g (Saturated 6g); Cholesterol 50mg; Sodium 1160mg; Carbohydrate 53g (Dietary Fiber 3g); Protein 23g
% Daily Value: Vitamin A 4%; Vitamin C 10%; Calcium 6%; Iron 20%
Diet Exchanges: 3 Starch, 1 1/2 Medium-Fat Meat, 2 Vegetable, 3 Fat

Betty's Tip

For an even quicker dinner-fix, microwave the chicken breast patties instead of using conventional directions.

Garlic Ranch
Pita

PREP: 5 MIN ▪ 4 SANDWICHES

I cup shredded lettuce

1/2 pound sliced cooked deli turkey

I can (4 ounces) chopped green chilies, drained

4 pita breads (6 inches in diameter), cut in half to form pockets

1/4 cup garlic ranch dressing

Place lettuce, turkey and chilies in pita bread halves. Top with dressing.

1 Serving: Calories 265 (Calories from Fat 80); Fat 9g (Saturated 2g); Cholesterol 30mg; Sodium 1120mg; Carbohydrate 33g (Dietary Fiber 2g); Protein 15g
% Daily Value: Vitamin A 2%; Vitamin C 16%; Calcium 8%; Iron 10%
Diet Exchanges: 2 Starch, 1 Lean Meat, 1 Fat

Red Pepper
Turkey Rolls

PREP: 10 MIN ▪ COOK: 5 MIN ▪ 4 SERVINGS

4 uncooked turkey breast slices, 1/4 inch thick

1/4 teaspoon salt

1/4 teaspoon pepper

1/2 medium red pepper, cut into 8 strips

4 green onions, 4 inches long

2 tablespoons oil

1/2 cup country Dijon chicken sauté (from 9.2 ounce bottle)

Season both sides of turkey slices with salt and pepper. Place slices on flat surface. Place 2 red pepper strips and one green onion piece across center of slice. Tightly roll turkey slice around peppers and onion, fasten with wooden pick.

Heat oil in 10-inch nonstick skillet over medium-high heat. Add turkey rolls to skillet and brown all sides of roll, about 2 minutes.

Add sauce and bring to a boil, cover, and reduce heat to medium. Cook for 2 to 3 minutes or until turkey is no longer pink, turning once.

1 Serving: Calories 280 (Calories from Fat 115); Fat 13g (Saturated 3g); Cholesterol 65mg; Sodium 920mg; Carbohydrate 16g (Dietary Fiber 1g); Protein 26g
% Daily Value: Vitamin A 12%; Vitamin C 26%; Calcium 2%; Iron 6%
Diet Exchanges: 1 Starch, 3 Lean Meat, 1 Fat

Italian Turkey
Pita

PREP: 5 MIN ■ 4 SANDWICHES

1/2 pound sliced cooked deli turkey ham

1 cup bite-size pieces assorted salad greens

1/2 cup shredded mozzarella cheese (2 ounces)

2 pita breads (6 to 8 inches in diameter), cut in half to form pockets

1/2 cup Italian dressing

Place turkey ham, salad greens and cheese in pita bread halves. Top with dressing.

1 Serving: Calories 355 (Calories from Fat 160); Fat 18g (Saturated 4g); Cholesterol 45mg; Sodium 1120mg; Carbohydrate 30g (Dietary Fiber 1g); Protein 19g
% Daily Value: Vitamin A 4%; Vitamin C 0%; Calcium 14%; Iron 16%
Diet Exchanges: 2 Starch, 2 Lean Meat, 2 Fat

Betty's Tip

Turkey ham looks like authentic ham made from pork and has the same smoky flavor, but turkey ham is lower in fat.

Garden Vegetable and Pasta Salad

PREP: 12 MIN ▪ CHILL: 10 MIN ▪ 4 SERVINGS

1 bag (16 ounces) frozen primavera vegetables with pasta

1 cup shredded cooked chicken

2 medium stalks celery, sliced (1 cup)

1/4 cup ranch dressing

Freshly ground pepper, if desired

Cook vegetables as directed on package. Stir in chicken, celery and dressing. Cover and refrigerate 10 minutes to cool. Sprinkle with pepper.

1 Serving: Calories 295 (Calories from Fat 155); Fat 17g (Saturated 5g); Cholesterol 40mg; Sodium 580mg; Carbohydrate 25g (Dietary Fiber 4g); Protein 15g
*% **Daily Value:*** Vitamin A 22%; Vitamin C 10%; Calcium 6%; Iron 2%
Diet Exchanges: 1 Starch, 1 Lean Meat, 2 Vegetable, 3 Fat

Try This

To change this easy main dish, how about using frozen creamy Cheddar vegetables with pasta or herb-seasoned vegetables with pasta?

Mediterranean
Chicken Salad

PREP: 6 MIN ■ 6 SERVINGS

2 cups diced cooked chicken

1 bag (10 ounces) ready-to-eat Italian-blend salad greens

1 can (14 ounces) artichoke hearts, drained and chopped

1 can (4 1/4 ounces) chopped ripe olives, drained

1/4 cup tomato-and-herb Italian dressing

Mix all ingredients except dressing in large bowl. Toss with dressing until coated.

1 Serving: Calories 195 (Calories from Fat 110); Fat 12g (Saturated 2g); Cholesterol 40mg; Sodium 500mg; Carbohydrate 11g (Dietary Fiber 5g); Protein 16g
% Daily Value: Vitamin A 14%; Vitamin C 30%; Calcium 6%; Iron 14%
Diet Exchanges: 2 Medium-Fat Meat, 2 Vegetable

Try This

The choices for salad dressings are endless. Try zesty Italian, Parmesan ranch, red wine vinaigrette or garlic ranch.

Chicken Caesar
Sandwiches

Prep: 5 min ▪ Cook: 15 min ▪ 4 servings

4 boneless, skinless chicken breast halves (about 1 1/4 pounds)

3 cups romaine pieces (from 10-ounce bag)

2 tablespoons grated Parmesan cheese

1/2 cup creamy Caesar dressing

1 round focaccia bread (12 inches in diameter)

Heat 12-inch nonstick skillet over medium-high heat. Cook chicken in skillet 12 to 15 minutes, turning once, until juice is no longer pink when centers of thickest pieces are cut. Toss romaine, cheese and 1/4 cup of the dressing.

Cut focaccia horizontally in half; cut into 4 wedges. Spread remaining 1/4 cup dressing over cut sides of focaccia. Place one-fourth of the romaine mixture and chicken breast half on bottom wedges. Top with top wedges.

1 Serving: Calories 715 (Calories from Fat 280); Fat 31g (Saturated 5g); Cholesterol 90mg; Sodium 1670mg; Carbohydrate 71g (Dietary Fiber 3g); Protein 41g
% Daily Value: Vitamin A 6%; Vitamin C 8%; Calcium 6%; Iron 32%
Diet Exchanges: 4 Starch, 3 Lean Meat, 2 Vegetable, 4 Fat

Betty's Tip

Serve a cold pasta or vegetable salad from the deli with these snazzy sandwiches.

Chicken and
Tortellini Salad

PREP: 12 MIN ▪ 6 SERVINGS

1 package (9 ounces) refrigerated cheese-filled tortellini

6 cups bite-size pieces assorted salad greens

3 cups chopped cooked chicken

1/2 cup Italian dressing

1/3 cup shredded Parmesan cheese

Cook and drain tortellini as directed on package. Mix tortellini and remaining ingredients except cheese. Sprinkle with cheese.

1 Serving: Calories 325 (Calories from Fat 190); Fat 21g (Saturated 6g); Cholesterol 100mg; Sodium 330mg; Carbohydrate 11g (Dietary Fiber 1g); Protein 24g
*% **Daily Value:** Vitamin A 10%; Vitamin C 8%; Calcium 12%; Iron 10%*
***Diet Exchanges:** 1/2 Starch, 3 Lean Meat, 1 Vegetable, 2 Fat*

Betty's Tip

To save time, look for precooked frozen salad tortellini in grocer's freezer case and packaged ready-to-eat salad greens.

Chapter 2

Stir-Fries and Skillet Meals

Spicy Chicken
with Broccoli

PREP: 25 MIN ▪ CHILL: 20 MIN ▪ COOK: 5 MIN ▪ 4 SERVINGS

1 pound chicken breast tenders

2 teaspoons cornstarch

1/2 teaspoon salt

1/4 teaspoon white pepper

1 pound broccoli

3 tablespoons chili oil or vegetable oil

1 jalapeño chili, cut into very thin slices

2 tablespoons brown bean sauce or dark soy sauce

2 teaspoons finely chopped garlic

1 teaspoon sugar

1 teaspoon finely chopped gingerroot

3 medium green onions, cut into 1-inch diagonal pieces

Mix chicken, cornstarch, salt and white pepper in medium bowl. Cover and refrigerate 20 minutes.

Peel outer layer from broccoli. Cut broccoli stems crosswise into thin slices; remove flowerets. Cut stems diagonally into 1/4-inch slices. Place broccoli flowerets and stems in boiling water; heat to boiling. Cover and boil 1 minute; drain. Immediately rinse in cold water; drain.

Heat wok or 12-inch skillet over high heat. Add oil; rotate wok to coat side. Add chili, brown bean sauce, garlic, sugar and gingerroot; stir-fry 10 seconds. Add chicken; stir-fry about 2 minutes or until chicken is no longer pink in center. Add broccoli and green onions; stir-fry about 1 minute or until broccoli is heated through.

1 Serving: Calories 260 (Calories from Fat 125); Fat 14g (Saturated 3g); Cholesterol 65mg; Sodium 440mg; Carbohydrate 10g (Dietary Fiber 2g); Protein 26g
% Daily Value: Vitamin A 20%; Vitamin C 74%; Calcium 6%; Iron 10%
Diet Exchanges: 3 Lean Meat, 2 Vegetable, 1 Fat

Betty's Tip

Wear plastic or latex gloves (or place your hands in plastic sandwich bags) when working with chilies to prevent the oils from irritating your skin or eyes. If you prefer a milder flavor, cut the chili in half and remove the membranes and seeds before slicing.

Chicken
Lo Mein

PREP: 8 MIN ▪ COOK: 8 MIN ▪ 4 SERVINGS

8 ounces uncooked linguine, broken in half

1 pound boneless, skinless chicken breasts, cut into thin strips

1/2 cup stir-fry sauce

1/4 cup chicken broth

1/4 teaspoon crushed red pepper

1 bag (16 ounces) frozen broccoli, carrots and cauliflower

Cook and drain linguine as directed on package. Spray 10-inch skillet with cooking spray; heat over medium-high heat. Add chicken; stir-fry 2 to 3 minutes or until brown. Add stir-fry sauce, broth and red pepper to chicken and stir. Heat to boiling. Stir in frozen vegetables. Heat to boiling; reduce heat. Simmer uncovered about 5 minutes or until chicken is no longer pink in center and vegetables are crisp-tender. Serve chicken mixture over linguine.

1 Serving: Calories 340 (Calories from Fat 35); Fat 4g (Saturated 1g); Cholesterol 35mg; Sodium 240mg; Carbohydrate 59g (Dietary Fiber 6g); Protein 23g
% Daily Value: Vitamin A 36%; Vitamin C 30%; Calcium 6%; Iron 20%
Diet Exchanges: 3 Starch, 1 Lean Meat, 3 Vegetable

Betty's Tip

Hankering for some beef? Use 1 pound beef boneless sirloin steak, cut into thin strips, instead of the chicken, and use beef broth instead of the chicken broth.

Mou Shu
Chicken

PREP: 12 MIN ■ COOK: 10 MIN ■ 4 SERVINGS

Plum Sauce (below)

1 tablespoon sesame or vegetable oil

1/2 pound cut-up boneless chicken breast for stir-fry

1/3 cup hoisin sauce

2 tablespoons grated gingerroot

3 tablespoons dry white wine or apple juice

1 teaspoon sugar

1 small head savoy cabbage, shredded (3 cups)

3 small carrots, shredded (1 cup)

8 flour tortillas (6 or 8 inches in diameter)

Prepare Plum Sauce. Heat oil in 10-inch skillet over medium-high heat. Cook chicken in oil 8 to 10 minutes, stirring occasionally, until no longer pink in center.

Stir in remaining ingredients except tortillas. Cook 4 to 6 minutes, stirring constantly, until cabbage is crisp-tender.

Warm tortillas as directed on package. Place about 1/3 cup chicken mixture on each tortilla; roll tortilla around filling. Serve with sauce.

1 Serving: Calories 335 (Calories from Fat 90); Fat 10g (Saturated 2g); Cholesterol 35mg; Sodium 680mg; Carbohydrate 46g (Dietary Fiber 5g); Protein 20g
% Daily Value: Vitamin A 62%; Vitamin C 22%; Calcium 12%; Iron 18%
Diet Exchanges: 2 Starch, 1 1/2 Very Lean Meat, 3 Vegetable, 1 Fat

Plum Sauce

1 cup sliced plums

1/4 cup plum jam

1 tablespoon white vinegar

Mix all ingredients in 1-quart saucepan. Cook over medium heat about 5 minutes, stirring occasionally, until plums are tender.

74 *Betty Crocker's* Best Chicken Cookbook

Try This

Can't find fresh plums?
Try chopping canned
plums for the sauce. You
may also be able to find
bottled plum sauce in the
Asian foods aisle, though
it will be smooth rather
than chunky.

Chicken and
Pasta Stir-Fry

2 cups uncooked farfalle (bow-tie) pasta (4 ounces)

1 pound asparagus, cut into 2-inch pieces (3 cups)

2 medium onions, sliced

1 1/2 cups chicken broth

1 pound boneless, skinless chicken breast halves, cut into 1-inch pieces

3 tablespoons chopped fresh or 1 tablespoon dried basil leaves

3 tablespoons chopped sun-dried tomatoes (not oil-packed)

1/4 teaspoon pepper

Freshly grated Parmesan cheese, if desired

Cook and drain pasta as directed on package.

Spray 12-inch skillet with cooking spray; heat over medium heat. Cook asparagus, onions and 1 cup of the broth in skillet 5 to 7 minutes, stirring occasionally, until liquid has evaporated. Remove mixture from skillet.

Spray skillet with cooking spray; heat over medium-high heat. Add chicken; stir-fry about 5 minutes or until no longer pink in center.

Return asparagus mixture to skillet. Stir in remaining 1/2 cup broth, the basil, tomatoes, pepper and pasta. Cook about 2 minutes, stirring frequently, until mixture is hot. Sprinkle with cheese.

1 Serving: Calories 290 (Calories from Fat 45); Fat 5g (Saturated 1g); Cholesterol 70mg; Sodium 510mg; Carbohydrate 31g (Dietary Fiber 3g); Protein 33g
*% **Daily Value:** Vitamin A 6%; Vitamin C 14%; Calcium 4%; Iron 16%*
***Diet Exchanges:** 2 Starch, 4 Very Lean Meat*

Betty's Tip

If you'd like to serve six, this is an easy recipe to stretch. Add more veggies, like broccoli flowerets or sliced carrots, and more pasta, too. For interest, use a different shape or color of pasta.

Chicken with
Garlic Bread Crumbs

PREP: 10 MIN ▪ COOK: 6 MIN ▪ 4 SERVINGS

1/2 cup seasoned dry bread crumbs

1/4 cup chopped fresh parsley or 1 tablespoon parsley flakes

1/4 teaspoon salt

2 cloves garlic, finely chopped

1 1/4 pounds boneless, skinless chicken breasts, cut into thin strips

1 egg, beaten

2 tablespoons margarine or butter

Spaghetti or barbecue sauce, warmed, if desired

Mix bread crumbs, parsley, salt and garlic. Dip chicken strips into egg, then coat with bread crumb mixture.

Melt margarine in 10-inch skillet over medium-high heat. Cook chicken in margarine 5 to 6 minutes, stirring occasionally, until no longer pink in center. Serve with spaghetti sauce.

1 Serving: Calories 265 (Calories from Fat 80); Fat 9g (Saturated 2g); Cholesterol 140mg; Sodium 400mg; Carbohydrate 11g (Dietary Fiber 0g); Protein 35g
*% **Daily Value:*** Vitamin A 8%; Vitamin C 4%; Calcium 6%; Iron 12%
Diet Exchanges: 1 Starch, 4 1/2 Very Lean Meat, 1 Fat

Try This

Out of fresh garlic? Use 1/4 teaspoon garlic powder instead.

Chicken and
Sweet Potato Curry

PREP: 15 MIN ▪ COOK: 18 MIN ▪ 4 SERVINGS

2 tablespoons all-purpose flour

1 tablespoon curry powder

1/2 teaspoon salt

1 pound boneless, skinless chicken breast halves, cut into 3/4- to 1-inch pieces

1 tablespoon vegetable oil

1 1/4 cups apple juice

2 cups cubed peeled sweet potatoes

1 fresh mild chili (about 3 to 4 inches in length), chopped

2 tablespoons apple jelly

Mix flour, curry powder and salt in heavy-duty resealable plastic bag. Add chicken; seal bag and shake until chicken is evenly coated.

Heat oil in 12-inch nonstick skillet over medium-high heat. Add chicken; stir-fry 2 to 3 minutes or until brown. Stir any remaining flour mixture into apple juice. Stir apple juice, sweet potatoes and chili into chicken.

Cover and cook 10 to 15 minutes, stirring occasionally, until chicken is no longer pink in center and potatoes are tender. Stir in jelly until melted.

1 Serving: *Calories 330 (Calories from Fat 70); Fat 8g (Saturated 2g); Cholesterol 70mg; Sodium 370mg; Carbohydrate 41g (Dietary Fiber 4g); Protein 27g*
% Daily Value: *Vitamin A 100%; Vitamin C 36%; Calcium 4%; Iron 12%*
Diet Exchanges: *2 Starch, 3 Very Lean Meat, 1 Fruit, 1/2 Fat*

Betty's Tip

Serve on a mound of hot, cooked couscous or rice. Top with chopped fresh chives, chutney or chopped peanuts or put them in small bowls and let everyone choose their own toppings.

Chicken and Apple-Rice Skillet

PREP: 8 MIN ▪ COOK: 20 MIN ▪ 4 SERVINGS

1 tablespoon margarine or butter

1 1/4 pounds boneless, skinless chicken breasts, cut into thin strips

1 large unpeeled tart eating apple, sliced

1 3/4 cups chicken broth

1 package (6.25 ounces) fast-cooking long grain and wild rice mix

Additional apple slices, if desired

Melt margarine in 12-inch skillet over medium heat. Cook chicken and apple in margarine 10 to 12 minutes, stirring occasionally, until chicken is no longer pink in center.

Stir in broth and rice. Heat to boiling; reduce heat to low. Cover and simmer about 5 minutes or until rice is tender. Top with additional apple slices.

1 Serving: Calories 250 (Calories from Fat 65); Fat 7g (Saturated 2g); Cholesterol 70mg; Sodium 560mg; Carbohydrate 20g (Dietary Fiber 2g); Protein 29g
% Daily Value: Vitamin A 4%; Vitamin C 2%; Calcium 2%; Iron 8%
Diet Exchanges: 1 1/2 Starch, 3 1/2 Very Lean Meat

Try This

Use Granny Smith, Braeburn, Haralson or Pippin apples for a tart flavor and a crisp texture.

Pesto Ravioli
with Chicken

PREP: 15 MIN ▪ COOK: 15 MIN ▪ 4 SERVINGS

2 teaspoons olive or vegetable oil

1 package (15 ounces) chicken breast tenders

3/4 cup chicken broth

1 package (9 ounces) refrigerated cheese-filled ravioli

3 small zucchini, cut into 1/4-inch slices

1 large red bell pepper, thinly sliced

1/4 cup pesto

Freshly grated Parmesan cheese, if desired

Heat oil in 12-inch skillet over medium-high heat. Cook chicken in oil about 4 minutes, turning occasionally, until brown. Remove chicken from skillet.

Add broth and ravioli to skillet. Heat to boiling; reduce heat. Cover and simmer about 4 minutes or until ravioli are tender.

Stir zucchini, bell pepper and chicken into ravioli. Cook over medium-high heat about 3 minutes, stirring occasionally, until vegetables are crisp-tender and chicken is no longer pink in center. Toss with pesto. Sprinkle with cheese.

1 Serving: *Calories 355 (Calories from Fat 160); Fat 18g (Saturated 5g); Cholesterol 130mg; Sodium 890mg; Carbohydrate 17g (Dietary Fiber 3g); Protein 34g*
*% **Daily Value:** Vitamin A 32%; Vitamin C 72%; Calcium 18%; Iron 14%*
Diet Exchanges: 1 Starch, 4 Lean Meat, 1 Fat

Betty's Tip

Be sure to use a 12-inch skillet or you'll have a difficult time tossing all the ingredients. A Dutch oven can be used too, if you don't have a large skillet.

Easy Chicken
Alfredo

Prep: 10 min ▪ Cook: 11 min ▪ 4 servings

2 tablespoons olive or vegetable oil

1 1/4 pounds boneless, skinless, chicken breasts, cut into thin strips

2 medium zucchini, sliced (4 cups)

1 large red bell pepper, cut into thin strips (1 cup)

1 container (10 ounces) refrigerated Alfredo sauce

Grated fresh Parmesan cheese

Heat oil in 12-inch skillet over medium-high heat. Cook chicken in oil 5 to 6 minutes, stirring occasionally, until chicken is no longer pink in center. Add zucchini and bell pepper; cook about 5 minutes, stirring frequently, until vegetables are crisp-tender. Stir in Alfredo sauce. Sprinkle with cheese.

1 Serving: Calories 575 (Calories from Fat 370); Fat 41g (Saturated 21g); Cholesterol 165mg; Sodium 570mg; Carbohydrate 15g (Dietary Fiber 3g); Protein 39g
% Daily Value: Vitamin A 52%; Vitamin C 80%; Calcium 36%; Iron 12%
Diet Exchanges: 1 Starch, 5 Lean Meat, 5 Fat

Try This

You can make this meal lots of times with different flavored sauces. Try experimenting with some of the refrigerated sauces available, such as marinara, sun-dried tomato pesto or clam sauce.

Chicken with *Potato Pierogies*

PREP: 10 MIN ▪ COOK: 30 MIN ▪ 6 SERVINGS

1 package (16 ounces) frozen potato-filled pierogies

2 tablespoons margarine or butter

6 boneless, skinless chicken breast halves (about 1 3/4 pounds)

1/2 cup chicken broth

1/4 cup half-and-half

1/4 cup chopped fresh parsley

1/4 teaspoon salt

1 can (4 ounces) sliced mushrooms, drained

Cook and drain pierogies as directed on package. Melt margarine in 12-inch skillet over medium-high heat. Cook chicken in margarine about 5 minutes, turning once, until light brown. Add broth. Cover and cook 15 to 20 minutes or until juice of chicken is no longer pink when centers of thickest pieces are cut.

Add potato pierogies and remaining ingredients to chicken. Cook uncovered about 5 minutes or until hot.

1 Serving: Calories 285 (Calories from Fat 80); Fat 9g (Saturated 3g); Cholesterol 105mg; Sodium 550mg; Carbohydrate 19g (Dietary Fiber 1g); Protein 33g
*% **Daily Value:** Vitamin A 8%; Vitamin C 2%; Calcium 4%; Iron 12%*
***Diet Exchanges:** 1 Starch, 4 Lean Meat*

Try This

Pierogies are potato-filled dumplings. If you can't find them, you can easily use frozen cooked gnocchi to make Chicken with Potato Gnocchi.

Chicken Paprikash
with Dill Sour Cream

PREP: 18 MIN ■ COOK: 35 MIN ■ 6 SERVINGS

Dill Sour Cream (below)

2 tablespoons olive or vegetable oil

3- to 3 1/2-pound cut-up broiler-fryer chicken, skin removed

1 medium onion, chopped (1/2 cup)

1 Anaheim or banana chili, seeded and chopped

1 large tomato, chopped (1 cup)

1/2 cup sweet (Hungarian) paprika

1 teaspoon salt

1 clove garlic, finely chopped

3 cups hot cooked egg noodles

Prepare Dill Sour Cream.

Heat oil in 12-inch skillet or Dutch oven over medium heat. Cook chicken in oil 15 minutes, turning once, until brown on all sides.

Stir in onion, chili, tomato, paprika, salt and garlic. Cover and cook over low heat about 20 minutes or until juice of chicken is no longer pink when centers of thickest pieces are cut. Stir in Dill Sour Cream. Cook about 1 minute or until hot. Serve chicken mixture over noodles.

1 Serving: Calories 425 (Calories from Fat 190); Fat 21g (Saturated 7g); Cholesterol 130mg; Sodium 500mg; Carbohydrate 30g (Dietary Fiber 3g); Protein 32g
% Daily Value: Vitamin A 72%; Vitamin C 22%; Calcium 8%; Iron 26%
Diet Exchanges: 1 Starch, 3 Lean Meat, 3 Vegetable, 2 Fat

Dill Sour Cream

1 cup sour cream

2 tablespoons chopped fresh or 2 teaspoons dried dill weed

Mix ingredients. Cover and refrigerate until ready to use.

Lemon-Pistachio
Chicken

PREP: 5 MIN ■ COOK: 20 MIN ■ 4 SERVINGS

4 boneless, skinless chicken breast halves (about 1 1/4 pounds)

1 teaspoon lemon pepper

1 tablespoon vegetable oil

3 tablespoons lemon juice

1 teaspoon grated lemon peel

1/4 cup chopped pistachio nuts, toasted*

Lemon slices

Flatten each chicken breast half to 1/4-inch thickness between sheets of plastic wrap or waxed paper. Sprinkle both sides of chicken with lemon pepper.

Heat oil in 12-inch skillet over medium-high heat. Cook chicken, lemon juice and lemon peel in oil 10 to 15 minutes, turning chicken once and stirring juice mixture occasionally, until juice of chicken is no longer pink when centers of thickest pieces are cut. Serve chicken topped with any remaining pan juices, nuts and lemon slices.

1 Serving: Calories 225 (Calories from Fat 90); Fat 10g (Saturated 2g); Cholesterol 85mg; Sodium 160mg; Carbohydrate 3g (Dietary Fiber 1g); Protein 32g
% **Daily Value:** Vitamin A 0%; Vitamin C 2%; Calcium 2%; Iron 8%
Diet Exchanges: 4 Lean Meat

*To toast nuts, bake uncovered in ungreased shallow pan in 350° oven about 10 minutes, stirring occasionally, until golden brown. Or cook in ungreased heavy skillet over medium-low heat 5 to 7 minutes, stirring frequently until browning begins, then stirring constantly until golden brown.

Betty's Tip

Hot cooked rice and cooked baby-cut carrots or broccoli are the perfect accompaniments for this lemony nutty chicken.

Two-Pepper Chicken
with Honey Butter

PREP: 8 MIN ▪ COOK: 20 MIN ▪ 4 SERVINGS

4 boneless, skinless chicken breast halves (about 1 1/4 pounds)

1 tablespoon black peppercorns, crushed

1 tablespoon white peppercorns, crushed

1 tablespoon vegetable oil

1/4 cup margarine or butter, softened

2 tablespoons honey

Coat both sides of chicken with peppercorns. Heat oil in 10-inch skillet over medium-high heat. Cook chicken in oil 15 to 20 minutes, turning once, until juice is no longer pink when centers of thickest pieces are cut.

Mix margarine and honey. Top chicken with honey-margarine mixture.

1 Serving: Calories 320 (Calories from Fat 170); Fat 19g (Saturated 9g); Cholesterol 105mg; Sodium 140mg; Carbohydrate 10g (Dietary Fiber 0g); Protein 27g
% Daily Value: Vitamin A 10%; Vitamin C 0%; Calcium 2%; Iron 6%
Diet Exchanges: 1/2 Starch, 3 1/2 Lean Meat, 2 Fat

Betty's Tip

How do you crush peppercorns? It's easy using a mortar and pestle, mini-food processor, or spice or coffee grinder. Or place them in a resealable plastic bag and pound with a meat mallet or rolling pin.

Moroccan Spiced *Chicken*

<small>PREP: 10 MIN ■ COOK: 20 MIN ■ 4 SERVINGS</small>

1 tablespoon paprika

1/2 teaspoon salt

1/2 teaspoon ground cumin

1/4 teaspoon ground allspice

1/4 teaspoon ground cinnamon

4 boneless, skinless chicken breast halves (about 1 1/4 pounds)

1 tablespoon vegetable oil

1 small papaya, sliced

Mix paprika, salt, cumin, allspice and cinnamon. Coat both sides of chicken with spice mixture.

Heat oil in 10-inch skillet over medium heat. Cook chicken in oil 15 to 20 minutes, turning once, until no longer pink when centers of thickest pieces are cut. Serve chicken with papaya.

1 Serving: Calories 195 (Calories from Fat 70); Fat 8g (Saturated 2g); Cholesterol 75mg; Sodium 360mg; Carbohydrate 5g (Dietary Fiber 1g); Protein 27g
% Daily Value: Vitamin A 12%; Vitamin C 20%; Calcium 2%; Iron 8%
Diet Exchanges: 3 1/2 Very Lean Meat, 1 Vegetable, 1 Fat

Betty's Tip

Dress up this dish for entertaining by serving hot, cooked couscous with some raisins tossed in and Middle Eastern flatbread.

Tandoori Chicken
and Chutney

PREP: 5 MIN ▪ MARINATE: 1 HR ▪ COOK: 20 MIN ▪ 4 SERVINGS

Spicy Yogurt Marinade (below)

4 boneless, skinless chicken breast halves (about 1 1/4 pounds)

1/2 cup mango chutney

Hot cooked basmati rice, if desired

Prepare Spicy Yogurt Marinade. Place chicken in shallow glass or plastic dish. Pour yogurt mixture over chicken. Cover and refrigerate 1 hour.

Cook chicken and yogurt mixture in 12-inch skillet over medium-high heat 15 to 20 minutes, turning chicken once, until juice of chicken is no longer pink when centers of thickest pieces are cut. Top with chutney. Serve with rice.

1 Serving: Calories 160 (Calories from Fat 35); Fat 4g (Saturated 1g); Cholesterol 75mg; Sodium 380mg; Carbohydrate 3g (Dietary Fiber 0g); Protein 28g
% Daily Value: Vitamin A 2%; Vitamin C 0%; Calcium 6%; Iron 6%
Diet Exchanges: 4 Very Lean Meat

Spicy Yogurt Marinade

1/2 cup plain yogurt

1 tablespoon lemon juice

2 teaspoons grated ginger-root

1/2 teaspoon paprika

1/2 teaspoon ground coriander

1/2 teaspoon salt

1/4 teaspoon ground red pepper (cayenne)

1/8 teaspoon ground cloves

Mix all ingredients.

Betty's Tip

Entertain your friends with this typical northern Indian meal by serving with traditional condiments, such as coconut, raisins, peanuts and chopped hard-cooked egg. You can find mango chutney in the condiment or ethnic food aisle of your supermarket.

Basil- and Prosciutto-
Stuffed Chicken

PREP: 14 MIN ▪ COOK: 18 MIN ▪ 4 SERVINGS

4 boneless, skinless chicken breast halves (about 1 1/4 pounds)

4 teaspoons Dijon mustard

4 thin slices prosciutto or fully cooked ham

1/4 cup shredded mozzarella cheese (1 ounce)

4 basil leaves

1 tablespoon vegetable oil

Make a horizontal cut in each chicken breast half to within 1/2 inch of ends, forming a pocket. Brush each pocket with 1 teaspoon mustard; fill with prosciutto, cheese and basil. Secure pockets with toothpicks.

Heat oil in 10-inch skillet over medium heat. Cook chicken in oil 12 to 18 minutes, turning once, until juice is no longer pink when centers of thickest pieces are cut.

1 Serving: Calories 215 (Calories from Fat 90); Fat 10g (Saturated 3g); Cholesterol 80mg; Sodium 380mg; Carbohydrate 1g (Dietary Fiber 0g); Protein 30g
% Daily Value: Vitamin A 2%; Vitamin C 0%; Calcium 6%; Iron 6%
Diet Exchanges: 4 Lean Meat

Betty's Tip

Here's a great shortcut for making this recipe if you don't want to cut a pocket in the chicken: Cook chicken breasts in oil about 6 minutes, then turn, brush with mustard and top with prosciutto. Cook 6 to 8 minutes longer or until juice is no longer pink when centers of thickest pieces are cut. Place cheese and basil leaves on chicken; cook about 2 minutes or until cheese is melted.

Chicken in Brandy
Cream Sauce

PREP: 10 MIN ▪ COOK: 22 MIN ▪ 4 SERVINGS

1 tablespoon olive or vegetable oil

4 boneless, skinless chicken breast halves (about 1 1/4 pounds)

1 package (8 ounces) sliced mushrooms (3 cups)

4 medium green onions, chopped (1/4 cup)

1/4 teaspoon salt

1/4 cup brandy or chicken broth

1/2 cup whipping (heavy) cream

Hot cooked spinach fettuccine or regular fettuccine, if desired

Heat oil in 10-inch skillet over medium-high heat. Cook chicken in oil 10 to 15 minutes, turning once, until chicken is no longer pink when centers of thickest pieces are cut.

Stir in mushrooms, onions, salt and brandy. Cook 4 to 5 minutes or until mushrooms are tender and most of the liquid has evaporated. Gradually stir in whipping cream. Cook about 2 minutes or until hot. Serve over fettuccine.

1 Serving: Calories 290 (Calories from Fat 155); Fat 17g (Saturated 7g); Cholesterol 105mg; Sodium 230mg; Carbohydrate 5g (Dietary Fiber 1g); Protein 29g
% Daily Value: Vitamin A 8%; Vitamin C 4%; Calcium 4%; Iron 10%
Diet Exchanges: 4 Lean Meat, 1 Vegetable,1 Fat

Cornmeal Chicken
with Fresh Peach Salsa

PREP: 10 MIN ▪ COOK: 20 MIN ▪ 4 SERVINGS

Fresh Peach Salsa (below)

1/2 cup yellow cornmeal

1/2 teaspoon salt

1/4 teaspoon pepper

4 boneless, skinless chicken breast halves (about 1 1/4 pounds)

2 tablespoons vegetable oil

Prepare Fresh Peach Salsa.

Mix cornmeal, salt and pepper. Coat chicken with cornmeal mixture. Heat oil in 10-inch skillet over medium-high heat. Cook chicken in oil 15 to 20 minutes, turning once, until juice is no longer pink when centers of thickest pieces are cut. Serve with Peach Salsa.

1 Serving: Calories 405 (Calories from Fat 170); Fat 5g (Saturated 3g); Cholesterol 85mg; Sodium 520mg; Carbohydrate 31g (Dietary Fiber 5g); Protein 33g
% Daily Value: Vitamin A 12%; Vitamin C 30%; Calcium 2%; Iron 12%
Diet Exchanges: 5 Lean Meat, 2 Fruit, 1 Fat

Fresh Peach Salsa

3 cups chopped peeled peaches

1 large tomato, chopped (1 cup)

1/4 cup chopped fresh cilantro

3 tablespoons vegetable oil

2 tablespoons white vinegar

1/4 teaspoon salt

Mix all ingredients.

Betty's Tip

Three cups of chopped frozen (thawed) sliced peaches can be substituted for the fresh peaches.

Chicken
Nicoise

PREP: 10 MIN ▪ COOK: 25 MIN ▪ 4 SERVINGS

1 1/4 cups dry white wine or chicken broth

4 boneless, skinless chicken thighs (about 1 pound)

3 cloves garlic, finely chopped

1/2 cup frozen pearl onions

1 tablespoon Italian seasoning

2 medium bell peppers, sliced

6 Kalamata olives, pitted and chopped

2 cups hot cooked rice

Heat 1/4 cup of the wine to boiling in 10-inch nonstick skillet. Cook chicken in wine, turning once, until brown. Remove chicken from skillet; keep warm.

Add garlic, onions, Italian seasoning, bell peppers, olives and remaining 1 cup wine to skillet. Heat to boiling; boil 5 minutes.

Add chicken to skillet; reduce heat to medium. Cook 10 to 15 minutes or until juice of chicken is no longer pink when centers of thickest pieces are cut. Serve over rice.

1 Serving: Calories 330 (Calories from Fat 90); Fat 10g (Saturated 3g); Cholesterol 70mg; Sodium 125mg; Carbohydrate 32g (Dietary Fiber 2g); Protein 27g
% Daily Value: Vitamin A 4%; Vitamin C 46%; Calcium 6%; Iron 24%
Diet Exchanges: 2 Starch, 3 Lean Meat

Caesar Chicken
with Orzo

Prep: 5 min ■ Cook: 25 min ■ 4 servings

1 tablespoon vegetable oil

4 boneless, skinless chicken breast halves (about 1 1/4 pounds)

1 can (14 1/2 ounces) ready-to-serve chicken broth

1 cup water

1 cup uncooked rosamarina (orzo) pasta

1 bag (16 ounces) frozen broccoli, green beans, pearl onions and red peppers

3 tablespoons Caesar dressing

1/8 teaspoon coarsely ground pepper

Heat oil in 10-inch skillet over medium-high heat. Cook chicken in oil about 10 minutes, turning once, until brown. Remove chicken from skillet; keep warm.

Add broth and water to skillet; heat to boiling. Stir in pasta; heat to boiling. Cook uncovered 8 to 10 minutes, stirring occasionally, until pasta is tender. Stir in frozen vegetables (cut any large broccoli pieces in half) and dressing. Add chicken. Sprinkle with pepper.

Heat to boiling; reduce heat. Simmer uncovered about 5 minutes or until vegetables are crisp-tender and juice of chicken is no longer pink when centers of thickest pieces are cut.

1 Serving: *Calories 370 (Calories from Fat 115); Fat 13g (Saturated 2g); Cholesterol 70mg; Sodium 680mg; Carbohydrate 34g (Dietary Fiber 4g); Protein 33g*
*% **Daily Value:** Vitamin A 16%; Vitamin C 42%; Calcium 6%; Iron 16%*
***Diet Exchanges:** 2 Starch, 3 1/2 Lean Meat, 1 Vegetable*

Betty's Tip

For a lighter take on this terrific dish, don't use the oil; spray the pan with cooking spray instead and substitute reduced-fat Caesar dressing. You'll save 6 grams of fat and 65 calories per serving!

Skillet Chicken
Parmigiana

PREP: 10 MIN ▪ COOK: 15 MIN ▪ 4 SERVINGS

4 boneless, skinless chicken breast halves (about 1 1/4 pounds)

1/3 cup Italian-style dry bread crumbs

1/3 cup grated Parmesan cheese

1 egg, beaten

2 tablespoons olive or vegetable oil

2 cups spaghetti sauce

1/2 cup shredded mozzarella cheese (2 ounces)

Flatten each chicken breast half to 1/4-inch thickness between sheets of plastic wrap or waxed paper. Mix bread crumbs and Parmesan cheese. Dip chicken into egg, then coat with bread crumb mixture.

Heat oil in 12-inch skillet over medium heat. Cook chicken in oil 10 to 15 minutes, turning once, until juice is no longer pink when centers of thickest pieces are cut. Pour spaghetti sauce around chicken in saucepan; heat until hot. Sprinkle mozzarella cheese over chicken.

1 Serving: Calories 440 (Calories from Fat 160); Fat 18g (Saturated 6g); Cholesterol 150mg; Sodium 980mg; Carbohydrate 31g (Dietary Fiber 2g); Protein 41g
% Daily Value: Vitamin A 14%; Vitamin C 14%; Calcium 26%; Iron 14%
Diet Exchanges: 2 Starch, 5 Lean Meat

Betty's Tip

Is company coming? Serve the chicken over steaming-hot spaghetti and top with spaghetti sauce and cheese.

Garlic-Soy *Chicken*

PREP: 6 MIN ▪ MARINATE: 20 MIN ▪ COOK: 24 MIN ▪ 4 SERVINGS

4 boneless, skinless chicken breast halves (about 1 1/4 pounds)

1/4 cup soy sauce

1/4 cup dry sherry or chicken broth

2 tablespoons packed brown sugar

1 tablespoon grated ginger-root

2 cloves garlic, finely chopped

1 bag (16 ounces) frozen stir-fry vegetables

Hot cooked rice, if desired

Flatten each chicken breast half to 1/4-inch thickness between sheets of plastic wrap or waxed paper. Place chicken in shallow glass or plastic dish. Mix soy sauce, sherry, brown sugar, gingerroot and garlic; pour over chicken. Cover and let stand 20 minutes.

Remove chicken from marinade. Heat marinade in 12-inch skillet over medium-high heat until hot. Cook chicken in marinade 15 to 20 minutes, turning once, until no longer pink in center.

Stir in vegetables. Cook 2 to 4 minutes, stirring frequently, until vegetables are tender. Serve chicken mixture over rice.

1 Serving: Calories 210 (Calories from Fat 35); Fat 4g (Saturated 1g); Cholesterol 75mg; Sodium 1010mg; Carbohydrate 16g (Dietary Fiber 3g); Protein 30g
*% **Daily Value:** Vitamin A 36%; Vitamin C 30%; Calcium 6%; Iron 12%*
***Diet Exchanges:** 4 Very Lean Meat, 3 Vegetable*

Betty's Tip

When buying garlic, look for firm, fresh-looking bulbs with papery, white husks. Avoid any soft garlic, or garlic that has sprouted. Store garlic in a cool, dry place with good ventilation.

Chicken in
Fresh Herbs

PREP: 8 MIN ▪ MARINATE: 30 MIN ▪ COOK: 20 MIN ▪ 4 SERVINGS

4 boneless, skinless chicken breast halves (about 1 1/4 pounds)

1/4 cup chopped fresh chervil leaves

1/4 cup chopped fresh tarragon leaves

1/2 cup dry white wine or chicken broth

1 tablespoon lemon juice

1/2 teaspoon salt

1 medium shallot, chopped

Cracked pepper, if desired

Place chicken in shallow glass or plastic dish. Mix remaining ingredients except pepper; pour over chicken. Cover and let stand 30 minutes.

Cook chicken and herb mixture in 10-inch skillet over medium-high heat 15 to 20 minutes, turning chicken once, until juice of chicken is no longer pink when centers of thickest pieces are cut. Sprinkle with pepper.

1 Serving: Calories 150 (Calories from Fat 35); Fat 4g (Saturated 1g); Cholesterol 75mg; Sodium 370mg; Carbohydrate 2g (Dietary Fiber 0g); Protein 27g
% Daily Value: Vitamin A 2%; Vitamin C 2%; Calcium 4%; Iron 8%
Diet Exchanges: 4 Very Lean Meat

Betty's Tip

Chervil is an herb with a sweet flavor reminiscent of onion and parsley. It looks very similar to Italian flat-leaf parsley, which can be used as a substitute for chervil if you have trouble finding it. The other herb in this recipe is tarragon, which has a delicate licorice flavor.

Chapter 3

Baked and Roasted Chicken

Roasted New Potatoes
and Chicken

Prep: 8 min ▪ Bake: 1 hr ▪ 4 servings

1 1/2 to 2 pounds broiler-fryer chicken pieces, skin removed

1 pound small red potatoes, cut into fourths

2 tablespoons chopped fresh or 2 teaspoons dried basil leaves

1 tablespoon chopped fresh or 1/2 teaspoon dried thyme leaves

3 tablespoons olive or vegetable oil

1 teaspoon garlic salt

Heat oven to 375°. Place chicken and potatoes in ungreased rectangular pan, 13×9×2 inches. Mix remaining ingredients; sprinkle over chicken and potatoes.

Cover and bake 30 minutes; turn chicken and potatoes. Bake uncovered 20 to 30 minutes longer or until juice of chicken is no longer pink when centers of thickest pieces are cut.

1 Serving: Calories 305 (Calories from Fat 135); Fat 15g (Saturated 3g); Cholesterol 60mg; Sodium 310mg; Carbohydrate 23g (Dietary Fiber 2g); Protein 21g
% Daily Value: Vitamin A 2%; Vitamin C 10%; Calcium 2%; Iron 12%
Diet Exchanges: 1 1/2 Starch, 2 Lean Meat, 2 Fat

Betty's Tip

New potatoes are young red or brown potatoes that are about 1 1/2 inches in diameter. Their texture is velvety, and their skins are very tender. Because the skins are so tender, these potatoes are usually not peeled.

Herb Chicken with *Roasted Garlic*

PREP: 12 MIN; BAKE: 1 HR ■ 6 SERVINGS

3- to 3 1/2-pound cut-up broiler-fryer chicken

1/2 cup dry white wine or chicken broth

1/4 cup lemon juice

1 tablespoon chopped fresh or 1 teaspoon dried thyme leaves

1 tablespoon chopped fresh or 1 teaspoon crumbled dried rosemary leaves

1 tablespoon chopped fresh or 1 teaspoon dried sage leaves

1/2 teaspoon salt

3 medium bulbs garlic

Heat oven to 375°. Place chicken in ungreased rectangular pan, 13×9×2 inches. Mix remaining ingredients except garlic; pour over chicken. Cut 1/2 inch off top of garlic bulbs. Place garlic, cut side up, in pan with chicken.

Cover and bake 30 minutes; turn chicken. Bake uncovered 20 to 30 minutes longer or until juice of chicken is no longer pink when centers of thickest pieces are cut. To serve, gently squeeze garlic out of cloves over chicken. Serve with pan juices.

1 Serving: Calories 235 (Calories from Fat 115); Fat 13g (Saturated 4g); Cholesterol 85mg; Sodium 280mg; Carbohydrate 2g (Dietary Fiber 0g); Protein 27g
*% **Daily Value:** Vitamin A 4%; Vitamin C 2%; Calcium 2%; Iron 8%*
***Diet Exchanges:** 4 Lean Meat*

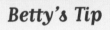

Betty's Tip

Did you know the longer garlic is cooked, the sweeter and milder it becomes? So you don't have to worry about this garlic being too strong when it is spread over the chicken. Roasted garlic is great spread on slices of crusty bread, too!

Crispy Chicken with *Apricot Stuffing*

PREP: 20 MIN ▪ BAKE: 1 HR ▪ 6 SERVINGS

Apricot Stuffing (below)

1 cup crushed cornflakes

1 tablespoon chopped fresh or 1 teaspoon dried thyme leaves

1/2 teaspoon salt

3- to 3 1/2-pound cut-up broiler-fryer chicken, skin removed

2 eggs, beaten

Heat oven to 375°. Grease rectangular pan, 13×9×2 inches. Prepare Apricot Stuffing. Spoon stuffing into pan. Mix cornflakes, thyme and salt in shallow dish. Dip chicken into eggs, then coat with cornflakes mixture. Place chicken on stuffing in pan.

Cover and bake 30 minutes; turn chicken. Bake uncovered 20 to 30 minutes longer or until juice of chicken is no longer pink when centers of thickest pieces are cut.

1 Serving: Calories 640 (Calories from Fat 305); Fat 34g (Saturated 7g); Cholesterol 160mg; Sodium 1100mg; Carbohydrate 52g (Dietary Fiber 4g); Protein 35g
% Daily Value: Vitamin A 36%; Vitamin C 6%; Calcium 8%; Iron 38%
Diet Exchanges: 3 Starch, 4 Lean Meat, 4 Fat

Apricot Stuffing

3/4 cup chopped pecans, toasted (page 92)

3/4 cup chopped dried apricots

1/4 cup margarine or butter, melted

1 cup hot water

1 medium onion, chopped (1/2 cup)

1 bag (8 ounces) herb stuffing mix

Mix all ingredients.

Betty's Tip

The easiest way to chop dried fruits is with kitchen scissors, so snip away! If the apricots are too sticky, try dipping the scissors into flour to keep the fruit from sticking to them.

Chicken with
Cider Glaze

PREP: 5 MIN ■ BAKE: 1 HR ■ 4 SERVINGS

2 to 2 1/2 pounds broiler-fryer chicken pieces, skin removed

1/2 teaspoon salt

1/4 teaspoon black peppercorns, crushed

1/2 cup apple cider

1/2 cup roasted-apple marinade or applesauce

Chopped fresh parsley, if desired

Heat oven to 375°. Place chicken in ungreased rectangular pan, 13×9×2 inches. Sprinkle with salt and pepper. Pour cider and marinade over chicken.

Cover and bake 30 minutes; turn chicken. Bake uncovered 20 to 30 minutes longer or until juice of chicken is no longer pink when centers of thickest pieces are cut. Sprinkle with parsley.

1 Serving: Calories 205 (Calories from Fat 65); Fat 7g (Saturated 2g); Cholesterol 80mg; Sodium 370mg; Carbohydrate 9g (Dietary Fiber 0g); Protein 26g
*% **Daily Value:** Vitamin A 0%; Vitamin C 0%; Calcium 2%; Iron 6%*
Diet Exchanges: 4 Very Lean Meat, 1/2 Fruit, 1 Fat

Betty's Tip

Roasted-apple marinade is a bottled fat-free dressing and marinade made from fresh apples that have been roasted and mixed with champagne vinegar, sugar and spices. It is deep brown in color with a toasty, savory apple flavor. Look for it along with the salad dressings or marinades in your grocery store.

Three-Herb
Chicken

Prep: 5 min ▪ Marinate: 3 hr ▪ Bake: 1 hr 15 min ▪ 4 servings

1/2 cup olive or vegetable oil

1/2 cup lime juice

2 tablespoons chopped fresh or 2 teaspoons dried basil leaves

2 tablespoons chopped fresh or 2 teaspoons dried oregano leaves

2 tablespoons chopped fresh or 2 teaspoons dried thyme leaves

1 teaspoon onion powder

1/4 teaspoon lemon pepper

4 chicken thighs (about 1 pound)

4 chicken drumsticks (about 1 pound)

Mix all ingredients except chicken thighs and drumsticks in resealable heavy-duty plastic bag or glass bowl. Add chicken; turn to coat with marinade. Seal bag or cover dish; refrigerate 3 to 4 hours, turning occasionally.

Heat oven to 375°. Grease rack of broiler pan. Remove chicken from marinade; reserve marinade. Place chicken on rack in broiler pan. Bake uncovered 30 minutes; turn chicken. Brush with marinade. Bake uncovered about 45 minutes longer or until juice of chicken is no longer pink when centers of thickest pieces are cut. Discard any remaining marinade.

1 Serving: Calories 425 (Calories from Fat 280); Fat 31g (Saturated 7g); Cholesterol 110mg; Sodium 120mg; Carbohydrate 2g (Dietary Fiber 0g); Protein 35g
% Daily Value: Vitamin A 4%; Vitamin C 4%; Calcium 4%; Iron 14%
Diet Exchanges: 5 Lean Meat, 3 Fat

Crunchy Garlic
Drumsticks

PREP: 17 MIN ▪ BAKE: 50 MIN ▪ 4 SERVINGS

3 tablespoons margarine or butter, melted

1 tablespoon milk

1 tablespoon chopped fresh chives or parsley

1/2 teaspoon salt

1/2 teaspoon garlic powder

2 cups corn flakes cereal, crushed (1 cup)

3 tablespoons chopped fresh parsley

1/2 teaspoon paprika

8 chicken drumsticks (about 2 pounds)

Cooking spray

Heat oven to 425°. Spray rectangular pan, 13×9×2 inches, with cooking spray.

Mix margarine, milk, chives, salt and garlic powder. Mix cereal, parsley and paprika. Dip chicken into margarine mixture, then coat lightly and evenly with cereal mixture. Place in pan. Spray chicken with cooking spray.

Bake uncovered 35 to 50 minutes or until juice of chicken is no longer pink when centers of thickest pieces are cut.

1 Serving: Calories 355 (Calories from Fat 180); Fat 20g (Saturated 5g); Cholesterol 85mg; Sodium 630mg; Carbohydrate 14g (Dietary Fiber 0g); Protein 30g
% Daily Value: Vitamin A 26%; Vitamin C 10%; Calcium 6%; Iron 36%
Diet Exchanges: 1 Starch, 4 Lean Meat, 1 Fat

Betty's Tip

If you want to save fat and calories, use 6 bone-less, skinless chicken breast halves instead of the drumsticks (this will serve 6). Also, use 1/4 cup skim milk instead of the melted margarine. You'll slash 19 grams of fat and 195 calories per serving.

Chicken Legs with *Vegetables*

PREP: 10 MIN ■ BAKE: 1 HR ■ 4 SERVINGS

8 chicken drumsticks or thighs (about 1 1/4 pounds), skin removed

1 pound Yukon gold potatoes, cut into fourths

1 medium red or green bell pepper, cut into strips

1 medium onion, cut into wedges

2 tablespoons chopped fresh or 2 teaspoons dried marjoram leaves

3 tablespoons olive or vegetable oil

1 teaspoon garlic salt

Heat oven to 375°. Place chicken, potatoes, bell pepper and onion in ungreased rectangular pan, 13×9×2 inches. Mix remaining ingredients; sprinkle over chicken and vegetables.

Bake uncovered 30 minutes; turn chicken. Bake uncovered 25 to 30 minutes longer or until juice of chicken is no longer pink when centers of thickest pieces are cut.

1 Serving: Calories 380 (Calories from Fat 160); Fat 18g (Saturated 4g); Cholesterol 90mg; Sodium 320mg; Carbohydrate 28g (Dietary Fiber 3g); Protein 30g
% Daily Value: Vitamin A 16%; Vitamin C 58%; Calcium 4%; Iron 22%
Diet Exchanges: 2 Starch, 3 1/2 Lean Meat, 1 Fat

Betty's Tip

Yukon gold potatoes are medium-size potatoes with thin yellow skins and golden yellow flesh. They have a mild, slightly sweet flavor and a smooth, moist texture.

Baked Lemon
Chicken

Prep: 15 min ▪ Stand: 15 min ▪ Bake: 25 min ▪ 4 servings

4 boneless, skinless chicken breast halves (about 1 1/4 pounds)

1 egg white

1 teaspoon water

1/4 cup all-purpose flour

1 teaspoon baking soda

1/4 to 1/2 teaspoon ground red pepper (cayenne), if desired

Cooking spray

Chinese Lemon Sauce (below)

1/2 lemon, cut into thin slices

1 medium green onion, chopped (1 tablespoon), if desired

Cut each chicken breast half crosswise in half. Mix egg white and water in medium glass or plastic bowl. Add chicken; turn chicken to coat both sides. Let stand 10 minutes.

Heat oven to 450°. Spray nonstick cookie sheet with cooking spray. Remove chicken from egg mixture; discard egg mixture. Mix flour, baking soda and red pepper in resealable plastic bag. Add 1 chicken piece at a time. Seal bag; shake to coat chicken. Place chicken on cookie sheet; spray with cooking spray about 5 seconds or until surface of chicken appears moist.

Bake uncovered 20 to 25 minutes or until juice of chicken is no longer pink when centers of thickest pieces are cut. While chicken is baking, prepare Chinese Lemon Sauce. Let chicken stand 5 minutes; cut each piece crosswise into about 5 slices. Pour sauce over chicken. Garnish with lemon slices and green onion.

1 Serving: Calories 270 (Calories from Fat 35); Fat 4g (Saturated 1g); Cholesterol 75mg; Sodium 640mg; Carbohydrate 29g (Dietary Fiber 0g); Protein 29g
*% **Daily Value:** Vitamin A 0%; Vitamin C 2%; Calcium 2%; Iron 8%*
***Diet Exchanges:** 2 Starch, 3 Very Lean Meat*

Chinese Lemon Sauce

1/4 cup sugar

1/3 cup chicken broth

1 teaspoon grated lemon peel

3 tablespoons lemon juice

2 tablespoons light corn syrup

2 tablespoons rice vinegar

1/4 teaspoon salt

1 clove garlic, finely chopped

2 teaspoons cornstarch

2 teaspoons cold water

Heat all ingredients except cornstarch and cold water to boiling in 1-quart saucepan, stirring occasionally. Mix cornstarch and cold water; stir into sauce. Cook and stir about 30 seconds or until thickened. Serve warm, or cover and refrigerate up to 2 weeks.

Jamaican Jerk
Chicken

PREP: 10 MIN ▪ BAKE: 30 MIN ▪ 4 SERVINGS

2 tablespoons chopped fresh or 2 teaspoons dried thyme leaves

1/2 teaspoon crushed red pepper

1/2 teaspoon salt

1/4 teaspoon ground allspice

4 boneless, skinless chicken breast halves (about 1 1/4 pounds)

1 cup sliced papaya

1 cup sliced mango

1 medium red onion, sliced

1 medium yellow bell pepper, cut into 1/4-inch strips

Heat oven to 375°. Grease rectangular pan, 13×9×2 inches. Mix thyme, red pepper, salt and allspice. Rub thyme mixture on chicken. Place chicken in pan. Arrange remaining ingredients around chicken. Bake uncovered 20 to 30 minutes or until juice of chicken is no longer pink when centers of thickest pieces are cut.

1 Serving: Calories 200 (Calories from Fat 35); Fat 4g (Saturated 1g); Cholesterol 75mg; Sodium 360mg; Carbohydrate 15g (Dietary Fiber 2g); Protein 28g
% Daily Value: Vitamin A 20%; Vitamin C 76%; Calcium 4%; Iron 8%
Diet Exchanges: 4 Very Lean Meat, 1 Fruit

Betty's Tip

Save time by purchasing precut papaya and mango. You can find these items in the refrigerated case with other fruit items or in the canned fruits section.

Honey-Glazed Chicken Breasts

PREP: 6 MIN ▪ BAKE: 50 MIN ▪ 6 SERVINGS

6 boneless, skinless chicken breast halves (about 1 3/4 pounds)

1/2 cup orange juice

1/2 cup honey

2 tablespoons lemon juice

1/4 teaspoon salt

Chopped fresh parsley, if desired

Heat oven to 375°. Grease rectangular pan, 13×9×2 inches. Place chicken in pan. Mix remaining ingredients; pour over chicken.

Cover and bake 20 minutes; turn chicken. Bake uncovered 20 to 30 minutes longer or until juice of chicken is no longer pink when centers of thickest pieces are cut. Sprinkle with parsley.

1 Serving: Calories 255 (Calories from Fat 35); Fat 4g (Saturated 1g); Cholesterol 75mg; Sodium 170mg; Carbohydrate 26g (Dietary Fiber 0g); Protein 29g
% Daily Value: Vitamin A 0%; Vitamin C 6%; Calcium 2%; Iron 6%
Diet Exchanges: 1 1/2 Starch, 4 Very Lean Meat

Betty's Tip

Come and eat! Serve with biscuits or corn bread muffins and a nice side of steamed veggies.

Two-Mustard
Chicken

PREP: 6 MIN ■ BAKE: 35 MIN ■ 8 SERVINGS

1/2 cup Dijon mustard

1/4 cup coarse-grained mustard

1/4 cup honey

8 boneless, skinless chicken breast halves (about 2 1/2 pounds)

Fresh thyme, if desired

Heat oven to 375°. Grease rectangular pan, 13×9×2 inches. Mix mustards and honey; spread on both sides of chicken. Place in pan.

Bake uncovered 25 to 35 minutes or until juice is no longer pink when centers of thickest pieces are cut. Garnish with thyme.

1 Serving: Calories 195 (Calories from Fat 45); Fat 5g (Saturated 1g); Cholesterol 75mg; Sodium 360mg; Carbohydrate 10g (Dietary Fiber 1g); Protein 28g
% Daily Value: Vitamin A 0%; Vitamin C 0%; Calcium 2%; Iron 8%
Diet Exchanges: 1/2 Starch, 4 Very Lean Meat

Betty's Tip

Mustard is made from the ground seeds of the mustard plant. Dijon mustard has the addition of white wine. Coarse- and whole-grained mustard contains whole mustard seeds and has a strong mustard and nutty flavor and a slightly chewy texture. Serve with one of the interesting varieties of winter squash that has been dotted with butter and sprinkled with chives.

Curry-Coconut Chicken
with Honey Mustard

PREP: 15 MIN ▪ BAKE: 18 MIN ▪ 6 SERVINGS

1/2 cup milk

1 egg, beaten

2 cups shredded coconut

2 teaspoons curry powder

2 pounds chicken breast tenders

1/2 cup honey

1/2 cup Dijon mustard

Heat oven to 375°. Grease jelly roll pan, 15 1/2 × 10 1/2 × 1 inch, or large cookie sheet. Mix milk and egg in bowl. Mix coconut and curry powder in shallow dish. Dip chicken into milk mixture, then coat with coconut mixture. Place in pan.

Bake uncovered 10 minutes; turn chicken. Bake uncovered 5 to 8 minutes longer or until no longer pink in center. Mix honey and mustard; serve with chicken.

1 Serving: *Calories 115 (Calories from Fat 45); Fat 5g (Saturated 3g); Cholesterol 30mg; Sodium 110mg; Carbohydrate 10g (Dietary Fiber 1g); Protein 9g*
% Daily Value: *Vitamin A 0%; Vitamin C 0%; Calcium 2%; Iron 4%*
Diet Exchanges: *1/2 Starch, 1 Lean Meat*

Betty's Tip

Our coconut tenders have a mild curry flavor. Add more curry powder if you love curry flavor.

Chicken
Tetrazzini

1 package (7 ounces) spaghetti, broken into thirds

1/4 cup margarine or butter

1/4 cup all-purpose flour

1/2 teaspoon salt

1/4 teaspoon pepper

1 cup chicken broth

1 cup whipping (heavy) cream

2 tablespoons sherry or water

2 cups cubed cooked chicken or turkey

1 can (4 ounces) sliced mushrooms, drained

1/2 cup grated Parmesan cheese

Heat oven to 350°. Cook and drain spaghetti as directed on package. Melt margarine in 2-quart saucepan over low heat. Stir flour, salt and pepper into margarine. Cook, stirring constantly, until mixture is smooth and bubbly; remove from heat. Stir in broth and whipping cream. Heat to boiling, stirring constantly. Boil and stir 1 minute. Stir in sherry, spaghetti, chicken, and mushrooms.

Pour spaghetti mixture into ungreased 2-quart casserole. Sprinkle with cheese. Bake uncovered about 30 minutes or until bubbly in center.

1 Serving: Calories 450 (Calories from Fat 235); Fat 26g (Saturated 11g); Cholesterol 90mg; Sodium 710mg; Carbohydrate 33g (Dietary Fiber 2g); Protein 23g
% Daily Value: Vitamin A 20%; Vitamin C 0%; Calcium 14%; Iron 12%
Diet Exchanges: 2 Starch, 2 1/2 Lean Meat, 4 Fat

Alfredo-Sauced
Chicken and Rice

PREP: 30 MIN ▪ BAKE: 1 1/4 HR ▪ 6 SERVINGS

I 1/2 cups cooked wild rice

I 1/2 cups cooked regular long grain rice

I jar (17 ounces) Alfredo sauce

1/2 teaspoon dried tarragon or marjoram leaves

1/8 teaspoon pepper

6 boneless, skinless chicken breast halves (about 1 3/4 pounds)

1/4 to 1/2 teaspoon seasoned salt

I 1/2 cups cut-up asparagus

I 1/2 cups sliced mushrooms (4 ounces)

1/3 cup sliced roasted red bell peppers (from 7-ounce jar)

Heat oven to 350°. Mix wild rice, regular rice, 3/4 cup of the Alfredo sauce, 1/4 teaspoon of the tarragon and the pepper in ungreased rectangular baking dish, 13×9×2 inches.

Spray 12-inch nonstick skillet with cooking spray; heat over medium-high heat. Sprinkle chicken with seasoned salt. Cook chicken in skillet 3 to 4 minutes, turning once, until brown. Place chicken on rice mixture.

Mix remaining Alfredo sauce, remaining tarragon, the asparagus, mushrooms and bell peppers. Spoon over chicken and rice. Cover and bake 1 hour until juice of chicken is no longer pink when centers of thickest pieces are cut.

1 Serving: Calories 535 (Calories from Fat 280); Fat 31g (Saturated 18g); Cholesterol 160mg; Sodium 550mg; Carbohydrate 29g (Dietary Fiber 2g); Protein 37g
% Daily Value: Vitamin A 26%; Vitamin C 18%; Calcium 24%; Iron 12%
Diet Exchanges: 2 Starch, 4 Medium-Fat Meat, 2 Fat

Betty's Tip

You will need about 1/2 cup of uncooked wild or regular long grain rice to equal 1 1/2 cups cooked rice.

Fiesta Chicken
Lasagna

PREP: 15 MIN ▪ BAKE: 40 MIN ▪ STAND: 10 MIN ▪ 8 SERVINGS

9 uncooked lasagna noodles (9 ounces)

2 jars (16 ounces each) thick-and-chunky salsa

1 package (12 ounces) frozen grilled chicken breast patties, thawed and cut into 1/2-inch slices

1 can (15 ounces) black beans, rinsed and drained

1/4 cup chopped fresh cilantro

3 cups shredded Monterey Jack cheese (12 ounces)

Cook and drain noodles as directed on package. Rinse noodles with cold water; drain.

Heat oven to 375°. Spread 1/4 cup of the salsa in ungreased rectangular baking dish, 13×9×2 inches. Layer with 3 noodles and one-third each of the chicken, beans, cilantro, salsa and cheese. Repeat 2 times with remaining noodles, chicken, beans, cilantro, salsa and cheese.

Cover and bake 20 minutes. Uncover and bake 15 to 20 minutes or until hot in center. Let stand 10 minutes before cutting.

1 Serving: Calories 375 (Calories from Fat 135); Fat 15g (Saturated 9g); Cholesterol 65mg; Sodium 790mg; Carbohydrate 38g (Dietary Fiber 6g); Protein 28g
% Daily Value: Vitamin A 20%; Vitamin C 18%; Calcium 40%; Iron 18%
Diet Exchanges: 2 Starch, 2 1/2 Lean Meat, 2 Vegetable, 1 Fat

Betty's Tip

Plan ahead! To make tomorrow's dinner tonight, cover the unbaked lasagna tightly with aluminum foil and refrigerate up to 24 hours. Bake as directed, but keep in mind you may need to bake it a little longer because it went into the oven from the refrigerator.

Chicken and Rice
with Autumn Vegetables

PREP: 15 MIN ▪ BAKE: 30 MIN ▪ 4 SERVINGS

1 package (6.9 ounces) chicken-flavored rice mix

2 cups 1 1/2-inch cubes butternut squash

1 medium zucchini, cut lengthwise in half, then crosswise into 3/4-inch slices

1 medium red bell pepper, cut into 1-inch pieces (1 cup)

4 boneless, skinless chicken breast halves (about 1 1/4 pounds)

2 cups water

1/2 cup garlic-and-herb spreadable cheese

Heat oven to 425°. Mix rice, contents of seasoning packet, squash, zucchini and bell pepper in ungreased rectangular pan, 13×9×2 inches.

Spray 10-inch skillet with cooking spray; heat over medium-high heat. Cook chicken in skillet 5 minutes, turning once, until brown. Remove chicken from skillet.

Add water to skillet; heat to boiling. Pour boiling water over rice mixture; stir to mix. Stir in cheese. Place chicken on rice mixture. Cover and bake about 30 minutes or until liquid is absorbed and juice of chicken is no longer pink when centers of thickest pieces are cut.

1 Serving: Calories 340 (Calories from Fat 125); Fat 14g (Saturated 7g); Cholesterol 105mg; Sodium 320mg; Carbohydrate 23g (Dietary Fiber 2g); Protein 32g
*% **Daily Value:** Vitamin A 76%; Vitamin C 58%; Calcium 8%; Iron 14%*
***Diet Exchanges:** 1 Starch, 4 Lean Meat, 2 Vegetable*

Try This

Buttercup squash can be used if butternut is not available. Butternut squash is a long, tan-colored squash with a bulbous end while the buttercup variety is round with a flat bottom and dark green color. Buttercup has a drier texture, but both are sweet tasting.

Chicken with Wild Rice and Cranberry Stuffing

PREP: 15 MIN ■ COOK: 50 MIN ■ ROAST: 1 1/2 HR ■ 6 SERVINGS

3/4 cup uncooked wild rice

1 3/4 cups chicken broth

1/2 cup coarsely chopped cranberries

1/4 cup orange juice

2 tablespoons packed brown sugar

1 teaspoon grated orange peel

1/2 teaspoon ground nutmeg

1 medium onion, chopped (1/2 cup)

1 medium stalk celery, thinly sliced (1/2 cup)

1/3 cup coarsely chopped pecans or slivered almonds, toasted (page 179)

3- to 3 1/2-pound whole broiler-fryer chicken

Heat wild rice and broth to boiling in 1 1/2-quart saucepan, stirring once or twice; reduce heat. Cover and simmer 30 minutes, stirring occasionally. Stir in remaining ingredients except pecans and chicken. Cover and simmer 10 to 20 minutes, stirring occasionally, until liquid is absorbed and vegetables are just tender. Stir in pecans.

Heat oven to 375°. Fill wishbone area of chicken with stuffing. Fold wings across back with tips touching. Fill body cavity lightly with stuffing. (Place any remaining stuffing in small ungreased baking dish; cover and refrigerate. Place in oven with chicken the last 30 minutes of roasting.) Tie or skewer drumsticks to tail. Place chicken, breast side up, on rack in shallow roasting pan. Insert meat thermometer so tip is in thickest part of inside thigh muscle and does not touch bone.

Roast uncovered about 1 1/2 hours or until thermometer reads 180° and juice of chicken is no longer pink when center of thigh is cut. The temperature in the center of the stuffing should be 165°.

1 Serving: Calories 395 (Calories from Fat 170); Fat 19g (Saturated 4g); Cholesterol 85mg; Sodium 390mg; Carbohydrate 27g (Dietary Fiber 3g); Protein 32g
*% **Daily Value:** Vitamin A 4%; Vitamin C 4%; Calcium 2%; Iron 12%*
__Diet Exchanges:__ 1 1/2 Starch, 3 1/2 Lean Meat, 1 Vegetable, 1 Fat

Betty's Tip

Wild rice is actually not a rice, but an aquatic grass native to North America that has a nutty, earthy flavor and chewy texture. It is more expensive than regular rice because of its more limited supply. Garnish platter with cranberries, strips of orange peel, and halved peaches.

Spice-Rubbed
Rock Cornish Hens

PREP: 5 MIN ▪ BAKE: 1 1/4 HR ▪ 4 SERVINGS

1 tablespoon olive or vegetable oil

1 teaspoon ground turmeric

1 teaspoon onion powder

3/4 teaspoon garlic powder

1/2 teaspoon seasoned salt

1/4 teaspoon paprika

1/4 teaspoon pepper

2 Rock Cornish hens (about 1 1/2 pounds each)

Heat oven to 350°. Rub hens with oil. Mix all remaining ingredients except hens. Rub turmeric mixture on skins of hens. Place hens, breast sides up, on rack in shallow roasting pan. Insert meat thermometer so tip is in thickest part of inside thigh muscle and does not touch bone.

Roast uncovered 1 to 1 1/4 hours or until thermometer reads 180° and juice is no longer pink when center of thigh is cut.

1 Serving: Calories 325 (Calories from Fat 215); Fat 24g (Saturated 6g); Cholesterol 150mg; Sodium 240mg; Carbohydrate 1g (Dietary Fiber 0g); Protein 26g
% Daily Value: Vitamin A 4%; Vitamin C 0%; Calcium 2%; Iron 8%
Diet Exchanges: 4 Medium-Fat Meat, Fat 1

Oven-Barbecued *Chicken*

PREP: 10 MIN ▪ BAKE: 1 HR ▪ 6 SERVINGS

3- to 3 1/2-pound cut-up broiler-fryer chicken

3/4 cup chili sauce or ketchup

2 tablespoons honey

2 tablespoons soy sauce

1 teaspoon ground mustard (dry)

1/2 teaspoon prepared horseradish

1/2 teaspoon red pepper sauce

Heat oven to 375°. Place chicken, skin sides up, in ungreased rectangular pan, 13×9×2 inches. Mix remaining ingredients; pour over chicken.

Bake uncovered 30 minutes. Spoon sauce over chicken. Bake uncovered about 30 minutes longer or until juice of chicken is no longer pink when centers of thickest pieces are cut.

1 Serving: Calories 285 (Calories from Fat 115); Fat 13g (Saturated 4g); Cholesterol 85mg; Sodium 800mg; Carbohydrate 16g (Dietary Fiber 1g); Protein 27g
% Daily Value: Vitamin A 8%; Vitamin C 4%; Calcium 2%; Iron 8%
Diet Exchanges: 1 Starch, 3 Lean Meat, 1 Fat

Betty's Tip

Prepared horseradish can be mild, as far as horse-radish goes, or it can be eye-watering hot! Look for it in the refrigerated section near refrigerated pickles or in the ketchup and mustard section of your supermarket.

Oven Chicken
Kiev

PREP: 20 MIN ■ FREEZE: 30 MIN ■ BAKE: 35 MIN ■ 6 SERVINGS

1/4 cup margarine or butter, softened

1 tablespoon chopped fresh chives or parsley

1 clove garlic, finely chopped

6 boneless, skinless chicken breast halves (about 1 3/4 pounds)

3/4 cups crushed cornflakes

2 tablespoons chopped fresh parsley

1/2 teaspoon paprika

1/4 cup buttermilk or milk

Mix margarine, chives and garlic. Shape mixture into rectangle, 3×2 inches. Cover and freeze about 30 minutes or until firm.

Heat oven to 425°. Spray square pan, 9×9×2 inches, with cooking spray. Flatten each chicken breast half to 1/4-inch thickness between sheets of plastic wrap or waxed paper.

Cut margarine mixture crosswise into 6 pieces. Place 1 piece on center of each chicken breast half. Fold long sides of chicken over margarine. Fold ends up; secure each end with toothpick.

Mix cornflakes, parsley and paprika. Dip chicken into buttermilk, then coat evenly with cornflakes mixture. Place chicken, seam sides down, in pan.

Bake uncovered about 35 minutes or until juice of chicken is no longer pink when centers of thickest pieces are cut. Remove toothpicks.

1 Serving: Calories 260 (Calories from Fat 110); Fat 12g (Saturated 3g); Cholesterol 85mg; Sodium 260mg; Carbohydrate 7g (Dietary Fiber 0g); Protein 31g
% Daily Value: Vitamin A 18%; Vitamin C 4%; Calcium 2%; Iron 18%
Diet Exchanges: 1/2 Starch, 4 Lean Meat

Crunchy Oven-Fried *Chicken*

PREP: 10 MIN ■ BAKE: 1 HR ■ 6 SERVINGS

1/4 cup margarine or butter

5 cups cornflakes

2 teaspoons paprika

1 teaspoon salt

1/4 teaspoon pepper

3- to 3 1/2-pound cut-up broiler-fryer chicken

Heat oven to 375°. Melt margarine in jelly roll pan, 15 1/2×10 1/2×1 inch, in oven.

Place cornflakes, paprika, salt and pepper in blender. Cover and blend on medium speed until mixture looks like fine crumbs. Dip chicken into melted margarine, then coat evenly with cornflakes mixture. Place chicken, skin sides up, in pan.

Bake uncovered 45 to 60 minutes or until juice is no longer pink when centers of thickest pieces are cut.

1 Serving: Calories 380 (Calories from Fat 190); Fat 21g (Saturated 5g); Cholesterol 85mg; Sodium 820mg; Carbohydrate 21g (Dietary Fiber 1g); Protein 28g
% Daily Value: Vitamin A 36%; Vitamin C 10%; Calcium 2%; Iron 48%
Diet Exchanges: 1 1/2 Starch, 3 Lean Meat, 2 Fat

Betty's Tip

For a lower-fat version, remove skin from chicken before dipping it into the melted margarine.

Skillet-Fried
Chicken

PREP: 20 MIN ■ COOK: 30 MIN ■ 6 SERVINGS

1/2 cup all-purpose flour

1 tablespoon paprika

1 1/2 teaspoons salt

1/2 teaspoon pepper

3- to 3 1/2-pound cut-up broiler-fryer chicken

Vegetable oil

Mix flour, paprika, salt and pepper. Coat chicken with flour mixture.

Heat oil (1/4 inch) in 12-inch nonstick skillet over medium-high heat. Cook chicken in oil about 10 minutes or until light brown on all sides; reduce heat to low. Turn chicken skin sides up.

Simmer uncovered about 20 minutes, without turning, until juice of chicken is no longer pink when centers of thickest pieces are cut.

1 Serving: Calories 335 (Calories from Fat 190); Fat 21g (Saturated 5g); Cholesterol 85mg; Sodium 670mg; Carbohydrate 9g (Dietary Fiber 1g); Protein 28g
*% **Daily Value**: Vitamin A 10%; Vitamin C 0%; Calcium 2%; Iron 10%*
***Diet Exchanges**: 1/2 Starch, 4 Lean Meat, 2 Fat*

Betty's Tip

To reduce the fat to 10 grams and the calories to 230 per serving, remove skin from chicken before cooking. Use 2 table-spoons oil and a nonstick skillet.

Chicken
Marsala

PREP: 10 MIN ■ COOK: 15 MIN ■ 4 SERVINGS

4 boneless, skinless chicken breast halves (about 1 1/4 pounds)

1/4 cup all-purpose flour

1/4 teaspoon salt

1/4 teaspoon pepper

2 tablespoons olive or vegetable oil

2 cloves garlic, finely chopped

1/4 cup chopped fresh parsley or 1 tablespoon dried parsley flakes

1 cup sliced fresh mushrooms

1/2 cup dry Marsala wine or chicken broth

Flatten each chicken breast half to 1/4-inch thickness between plastic wrap or waxed paper. Mix flour, salt and pepper. Coat chicken with flour mixture; shake off excess flour. Heat oil in 10-inch skillet over medium-high heat. Cook garlic and parsley in oil 5 minutes, stirring frequently.

Add chicken and brown each side. Add mushrooms and wine. Cook 8 to 10 minutes, turning once, or until chicken is no longer pink in center. Serve with hot cooked pasta if desired.

Serving Size: 1 Serving. Calories 255 (Calories from Fat 100); Fat 11g (Saturated 2g); Cholesterol 75mg; Sodium 220mg; Carbohydrate 11g (Dietary Fiber 1g); Protein 28g
*% **Daily Value:** Vitamin A 2%; Vitamin C 4%; Calcium 2%; Iron 10%*
Diet Exchanges: 4 Lean Meat, 2 Vegetable

Try This

Marsala is an amber-colored wine from Sicily, with a flavor similar too, but richer than sherry. Marsala can be sweet or dry. Dry Marsala is used for savory dishes and sweet Marsala is used mainly in desserts.

Easy Chicken
Pot Pie

PREP: 16 MIN ▪ BAKE: 40 MIN ▪ 6 SERVINGS

1 bag (16 ounces) frozen mixed vegetables

1 cup cut-up cooked chicken

1 jar (12 ounces) chicken gravy

2 cups shredded Cheddar cheese (8 ounces)

1 cup Bisquick® Original baking mix

1/4 cup milk

1/4 teaspoon dried thyme leaves

2 eggs

Heat oven to 375°. Heat frozen vegetables, chicken and gravy to boiling in 2-quart saucepan, stirring frequently; keep warm.

Stir remaining ingredients with fork until blended. Pour chicken mixture into ungreased 2 1/2-quart casserole. Spoon batter over chicken mixture; spread gently to cover. Bake uncovered 35 to 40 minutes or until crust is golden brown. Let stand 5 minutes before serving.

1 Serving: Calories 365 (Calories from Fat 190); Fat 21g (Saturated 10g); Cholesterol 130mg; Sodium 930mg; Carbohydrate 24g (Dietary Fiber 3g); Protein 24g
% Daily Value: Vitamin A 68%; Vitamin C 4%; Calcium 28%; Iron 14%
Diet Exchanges: 1 Starch, 2 Lean Meat, 1 1/2 Vegetable, 3 Fat

Betty's Tip

Serve this hearty pie with a purchased bag of Caesar salad mix. For a quick dessert, drizzle caramel ice cream topping over fresh apple slices.

Turkey
Divan

PREP: 35 MIN ▪ BROIL: 3 MIN ▪ 6 SERVINGS

2 packages (10 ounces each) frozen broccoli spears

1/4 cup margarine or butter

1/4 cup all-purpose flour

1/8 teaspoon ground nutmeg

1 1/2 cups chicken broth

1 cup grated Parmesan cheese

1/2 cup whipping (heavy) cream

2 tablespoons dry white wine or chicken broth

6 large slices cooked turkey breast, 1/4 inch thick (3/4 pound)

Cook and drain broccoli as directed on package; keep warm. While broccoli is cooking, melt margarine in 1-quart saucepan over medium heat. Stir flour and nutmeg into margarine. Cook, stirring constantly, until smooth and bubbly; remove from heat. Stir in broth. Heat to boiling, stirring constantly. Boil and stir 1 minute; remove from heat. Stir in 1/2 cup of the cheese, the whipping cream and wine.

Place hot broccoli in ungreased rectangular baking dish, 11×7×1 1/2 inches. Top with turkey. Pour cheese sauce over turkey. Sprinkle with the remaining 1/2 cup of the cheese.

Set oven control to broil. Broil with top 3 to 5 inches from heat about 3 minutes or until cheese is bubbly and light brown.

1 Serving: Calories 295 (Calories from Fat 170); Fat 19g (Saturated 8g); Cholesterol 70mg; Sodium 660mg; Carbohydrate 10g (Dietary Fiber 3g); Protein 24g
% Daily Value: Vitamin A 32%; Vitamin C 28%; Calcium 24%; Iron 10%
Diet Exchanges: 3 Lean Meat, 2 Vegetable, 2 Fat

Betty's Tip

If you don't have leftover
cooked turkey, use 6
large slices of turkey
(sliced about 1/4 inch
thick) from the deli.

Chicken à la King

PREP: 20 MIN ▪ COOK: 10 MIN ▪ 6 SERVINGS

1/2 cup margarine or butter

1 small green bell pepper, chopped (1/2 cup)

1 cup sliced mushrooms (3 ounces)

1/2 cup all-purpose flour

1/2 teaspoon salt

1/4 teaspoon pepper

1 1/2 cups milk

1 1/4 cups chicken broth

2 cups cut-up cooked chicken or turkey

1 jar (2 ounces) diced pimientos, drained

12 toasted bread triangles or 3 cups hot cooked rice

Melt margarine in 3-quart saucepan over medium-high heat. Cook bell pepper and mushrooms in margarine, stirring occasionally, until bell pepper is crisp-tender. Stir in flour, salt and pepper. Cook over medium heat, stirring constantly, until bubbly; remove from heat. Stir in milk and broth. Heat to boiling, stirring constantly. Boil and stir 1 minute. Stir in chicken and pimientos; cook until hot. Serve over toasted bread triangles.

1 Serving: Calories 360 (Calories from Fat 190); Fat 21g (Saturated 5g); Cholesterol 45mg; Sodium 820mg; Carbohydrate 26g (Dietary Fiber 1g); Protein 20g
% Daily Value: Vitamin A 28%; Vitamin C 16%; Calcium 12%; Iron 12%
Diet Exchanges: 1 Starch, 2 Medium-Fat Meat, 2 Vegetable, 1 Fat

Try This

Instead of using fresh mushrooms, you can use a 4-ounce can of mushroom pieces and stems, drained. For a little extra flavor, save the mushroom liquid and add it with the milk. To make Tuna à la King, use a 12-ounce can of tuna, drained, instead of the chicken.

Chicken
Fricassee

PREP: 10 MIN ■ COOK: 1 1/2 HR ■ 6 SERVINGS

1/4 cup margarine or butter

3- to 3 1/2-pound cut-up broiler-fryer chicken

2 cups water

2 medium carrots, sliced (1 cup)

1 medium onion, chopped (1/2 cup)

1 teaspoon salt

1/2 teaspoon dried thyme leaves

2 whole cloves

1 dried bay leaf

Parsley Dumplings (below)

3 tablespoons all-purpose flour

1/2 cup milk or water

1/8 teaspoon pepper

Melt margarine in Dutch oven or 12-inch skillet over medium-high heat. Cook chicken in margarine 15 to 20 minutes or until brown on all sides. Drain margarine from Dutch oven.

Stir water, carrots, onion, salt, thyme, cloves and bay leaf into chicken. Heat to boiling; reduce heat. Cover and simmer 40 to 50 minutes or until chicken is no longer pink when centers of thickest pieces are cut. Prepare Parsley Dumplings.

Remove chicken; keep warm. Remove bay leaf; discard. Mix flour, milk and pepper until smooth; pour into Dutch oven. Heat to boiling, stirring constantly. Boil and stir 1 minute; reduce heat. Return chicken to Dutch oven.

Drop dumpling dough by rounded tablespoonfuls onto hot chicken (do not drop directly into liquid). Cover tightly and cook 10 to 14 minutes or until dumplings are fluffy and dry on top.

1 Serving: Calories 490 (Calories from Fat 250); Fat 28g (Saturated 7g); Cholesterol 90mg; Sodium 1040mg; Carbohydrate 30g (Dietary Fiber 2g); Protein 32g
*% **Daily Value:*** Vitamin A 56%; Vitamin C 4%; Calcium 18%; Iron 16%
Diet Exchanges: 2 Starch, 3 1/2 Lean Meat, 3 Fat

Parsley Dumplings

1 1/4 cups all-purpose flour

2 tablespoons chopped fresh parsley

2 teaspoons baking powder

1/2 teaspoon salt

3 tablespoons margarine or butter

2/3 cup milk

Mix flour, parsley, baking powder and salt in medium bowl. Cut in margarine, using pastry blender or crisscrossing 2 knives, until mixture looks like fine crumbs. Stir in milk.

Chicken
Salad

PREP: 10 MIN ▪ 2 SERVINGS

1 1/2 cups chopped cooked chicken or turkey

1/2 cup mayonnaise or salad dressing

1 medium stalk celery, chopped (1/2 cup)

1 small onion, finely chopped (1/4 cup)

1/4 teaspoon salt

1/4 teaspoon pepper

Mix all ingredients.

1 Serving: Calories 300 (Calories from Fat 235); Fat 26g (Saturated 4g); Cholesterol 60mg; Sodium 360mg; Carbohydrate 3g (Dietary Fiber 1g); Protein 15g
% Daily Value: Vitamin A 2%; Vitamin C 0%; Calcium 2%; Iron 4%
Diet Exchanges: 2 Medium-Fat Meat, 3 Fat

Betty's Tip

Classic chicken salad can be used as a sandwich filling or to stuff a tomato. It's even wonderful all by itself served on a lettuce-lined plate with some cut-up fresh vegetables or fruits.

Salsa Arroz con Pollo

PREP: 15 MIN ■ BAKE: 1 1/2 HR ■ 6 SERVINGS

1 cup uncooked regular long grain rice

1 cup frozen whole kernel corn

1 can (14 1/2 ounces) ready-to-serve chicken broth

1 can (14 1/2 ounces) salsa-flavored tomatoes with green chilies, undrained

1 can (15 ounces) black beans, rinsed and drained

3 tablespoons all-purpose flour

1 teaspoon chili powder

1/2 teaspoon ground cumin

1/2 teaspoon salt

3- to 3 1/2-pound cut-up broiler-fryer chicken, skin removed if desired

Heat oven to 375°. Mix rice, corn, broth, tomatoes and beans in ungreased rectangular baking dish, 13×9×2 inches.

Mix flour, chili powder, cumin and salt in heavy-duty resealable plastic bag. Add chicken, 2 pieces at a time; seal bag and shake until chicken is evenly coated.

Arrange chicken, meaty sides up, on rice mixture in pan. Cover and bake 1 1/4 hours. Uncover and bake 10 to 15 minutes longer or until liquid is absorbed and juice of chicken is no longer pink when centers of thickest pieces are cut.

1 Serving: Calories 490 (Calories from Fat 135); Fat 15g (Saturated 4g); Cholesterol 85mg; Sodium 970mg; Carbohydrate 57g (Dietary Fiber 7g); Protein 39g
% Daily Value: Vitamin A 10%; Vitamin C 12%; Calcium 10%; Iron 28%
Diet Exchanges: 3 Starch, 4 Lean Meat, 2 Vegetable

Betty's Tip

A resealable plastic bag for coating the chicken saves cleanup and makes evenly coating the chicken a breeze!

Chapter 5

Fire up the Grill

Peanut-Glazed
Rock Cornish Hens

PREP: 10 MIN ▪ GRILL: 55 MIN ▪ 8 SERVINGS

4 Rock Cornish hens (3/4 to 1 pound each)

1/2 cup chunky peanut butter

1/4 cup dry white wine or chicken broth

2 tablespoons honey

1 tablespoon soy sauce

1/4 teaspoon ground red pepper (cayenne)

4 medium green onions, finely chopped (1/4 cup)

1/2 cup dry-roasted peanuts

Brush grill rack with vegetable oil. Heat coals or gas grill for direct heat. Cut each hen in half along backbone and breastbone from tail to neck, using kitchen scissors. Mix remaining ingredients except peanuts.

Cover and grill hens, skin sides down, 15 minutes. Turn hens; brush with peanut butter mixture. Cover and grill 20 to 40 minutes longer or until thermometer reads 180° and juice is no longer pink when center of thigh is cut. Top hens with peanuts.

1 Serving: Calories 425 (Calories from Fat 280); Fat 31g (Saturated 8g); Cholesterol 150mg; Sodium 250mg; Carbohydrate 8g (Dietary Fiber 2g); Protein 31g
% Daily Value: Vitamin A 4%; Vitamin C 0%; Calcium 2%; Iron 8%
Diet Exchanges: 1/2 Starch, 4 Lean Meat, 4 Fat

Betty's Tip

Company's coming! Serve these peanutty hens with grilled zucchini and fragrant basmati rice for an Indonesian adventure.

Greek Chicken with *Red Wine and Garlic*

PREP: 6 MIN ■ MARINATE: 1 HR ■ GRILL: 55 MIN ■ 4 SERVINGS

1 1/2 to 2 pounds broiler-fryer chicken pieces

1/2 cup dry red wine or chicken broth

2 tablespoons chopped fresh or 1 tablespoon dried basil leaves

1 tablespoon chopped fresh or 1 teaspoon dried mint leaves

3 tablespoons olive or vegetable oil

2 cloves garlic, finely chopped

1 jar (4 3/4 ounces) pitted Kalamata or ripe olives, drained

Place chicken in shallow glass or plastic dish. Mix remaining ingredients except olives; pour over chicken. Cover and refrigerate 1 hour.

Brush grill rack with vegetable oil. Heat coals or gas grill for direct heat. Remove chicken from marinade; reserve marinade. Cover and grill chicken, skin sides down, 5 to 6 inches from medium heat 15 minutes. Turn chicken; brush with marinade. Cover and grill 20 to 40 minutes longer, brushing occasionally with marinade, until juice of chicken is no longer pink when centers of thickest pieces are cut. Discard any remaining marinade. Serve chicken with olives.

1 Serving: Calories 270 (Calories from Fat 180); Fat 20g (Saturated 4g); Cholesterol 65mg; Sodium 360mg; Carbohydrate 3g (Dietary Fiber 1g); Protein 20g
% Daily Value: Vitamin A 4%; Vitamin C 0%; Calcium 4%; Iron 12%
Diet Exchanges: 3 Lean Meat, 1 Fat

Betty's Tip

Kalamata olives, known as the Cadillac of olives, are imported from Greece. The plump, purplish to black olives have a moist texture and a robust, wine-like flavor.

Honey-Pecan
Chicken

PREP: 15 MIN ▪ COOK: 5 MIN ▪ GRILL: 1 HR 20 MIN ▪ 4 SERVINGS

Honey-Pecan Sauce (below)

1/4 cup margarine or butter, melted

2 tablespoons lemon juice

2 tablespoons water

1/2 teaspoon Worcestershire sauce

1/4 teaspoon salt

1/8 teaspoon pepper

3- to 3 1/2-pound whole broiler-fryer chicken, cut into fourths

Heat coals or gas grill for direct heat.

Prepare Honey-Pecan Sauce. Mix remaining ingredients except chicken in small 1-quart saucepan. Cook over low heat 5 minutes, stirring occasionally. Mop or brush margarine mixture over chicken.

Cover and grill chicken, skin sides up, 5 to 6 inches from medium heat 25 to 35 minutes; turn. Mop with margarine mixture. Cover and grill 35 to 45 minutes longer, turning and mopping 2 or 3 times with margarine mixture, until juice of chicken is no longer pink when centers of thickest pieces are cut. Discard any remaining margarine mixture. Serve chicken with Honey-Pecan Sauce.

1 Serving: Calories 560 (Calories from Fat 340); Fat 38g (Saturated 9g); Cholesterol 130mg; Sodium 530mg; Carbohydrate 15g (Dietary Fiber 0g); Protein 40g
% Daily Value: Vitamin A 28%; Vitamin C 2%; Calcium 2%; Iron 10%
Diet Exchanges: 1 Starch, 5 Medium-Fat Meat, 2 Fat

Honey-Pecan Sauce

3 tablespoons honey

2 tablespoons margarine or butter, melted

2 tablespoons chopped pecans, toasted (see Betty's Tip)

2 teaspoons lemon juice

1 teaspoon mustard

Mix all ingredients. Makes about 1/2 cup.

Caesar Chicken and
Vegetables with Pasta

PREP: 15 MIN ▪ MARINATE: 30 MIN ▪ GRILL: 1 HR ▪ 6 SERVINGS

3- to 3 1/2-pound cut-up broiler-fryer chicken

2/3 cup Caesar dressing

1 medium red bell pepper, cut into 1-inch pieces

2 medium zucchini or yellow summer squash, cut into 1-inch pieces

1 medium red onion, cut into wedges

3 cups uncooked rotelle pasta (8 ounces)

Salt and pepper to taste

Try This

For a different flavor twist, substitute your favorite Italian or oil and vinegar dressing for the Caesar dressing.

Place chicken in shallow glass or plastic dish or heavy-duty resealable plastic bag. Pour 1/3 cup of the dressing over chicken; turn chicken to coat with dressing. Cover dish or seal bag and refrigerate, turning chicken occasionally, at least 30 minutes but no longer than 24 hours.

Heat coals or gas grill. Remove chicken from dressing; reserve dressing. Cover and grill chicken, skin sides up, 4 to 5 inches from medium heat 15 to 20 minutes. Turn chicken. Cover and grill 20 to 40 minutes longer, turning and brushing 2 or 3 times with dressing, until juice of chicken is no longer pink when centers of thickest pieces are cut. While chicken is grilling, continue with next step.

Thread bell pepper, zucchini and onion alternately on each of four 10-inch metal skewers, leaving 1/4-inch space between each piece. Brush with remaining 1/3 cup dressing. Cover and grill vegetables 4 to 5 inches from medium heat 15 to 20 minutes, turning and brushing twice with dressing, until vegetables are crisp-tender. Discard any remaining dressing. While chicken and vegetables are grilling, continue with next step.

Cook and drain pasta as directed on package. Remove vegetables from skewers. Toss vegetables and pasta, adding additional dressing if desired. Sprinkle with salt and pepper. Serve with chicken.

1 Serving: Calories 565 (Calories from Fat 225); Fat 25g (Saturated 5g); Cholesterol 90mg; Sodium 400mg; Carbohydrate 53g (Dietary Fiber 3g); Protein 35g
% Daily Value: Vitamin A 16%; Vitamin C 34%; Calcium 4%; Iron 20%
Diet Exchanges: 3 Starch, 3 Lean Meat, 2 Vegetable, 3 Fat

Blueberry
Chicken

PREP: 8 MIN ▪ GRILL: 25 MIN ▪ 4 SERVINGS

4 boneless, skinless chicken breast halves (about 1 1/4 pounds)

1/4 teaspoon salt

1/2 cup blueberry jam

2 tablespoons white vinegar

1 cup fresh or frozen (thawed, drained) blueberries

Brush grill rack with vegetable oil. Heat coals or gas grill for direct heat. Sprinkle chicken with salt. Mix jam and vinegar.

Cover and grill chicken 4 to 6 inches from medium heat 10 minutes; turn chicken. Cover and grill 10 to 15 minutes longer, brushing once with jam mixture, until juice of chicken is no longer pink when centers of thickest pieces are cut. Brush with jam mixture. Serve chicken with blueberries.

*1 **Serving:** Calories 290 (Calories from Fat 65); Fat 7g (Saturated 2g); Cholesterol 75mg; Sodium 225mg; Carbohydrate 31g (Dietary Fiber 1g); Protein 27g*
*% **Daily Value:** Vitamin A 2%; Vitamin C 14%; Calcium 2%; Iron 6%*
*Diet **Exchanges:** 1 Starch, 3 Lean Meat, 1 Fruit*

Betty's Tip

Serve these fruity chicken breasts with cooked couscous and parsley, broccoflower and baby pattypan squash.

Pesto-Chicken
Packets

PREP: 15 MIN ▪ GRILL: 25 MIN ▪ 4 SERVINGS

4 boneless, skinless chicken breast halves (about 1 1/4 pounds)

8 roma (plum) tomatoes, cut into 1/2-inch slices

4 small zucchini, cut into 1/2-inch slices

1/2 cup basil pesto

Heat coals or gas grill for direct heat. Place 1 chicken breast half, 2 sliced tomatoes and 1 sliced zucchini on 1 side of each of 4 sheets of heavy-duty aluminum foil, 18×12 inches. Spoon 2 tablespoons pesto over chicken mixture. Fold other half of foil over chicken and vegetables so edges meet. Seal edges, making a tight 1/2-inch fold; fold again. Allow space on sides for circulation and expansion. Repeat folding to seal each side.

Cover and grill packets 4 to 5 inches from medium heat 20 to 25 minutes or until juice of chicken is no longer pink when centers of thickest pieces are cut. Place foil packets on plates. To serve, cut a large **X** across top of packet; fold back foil.

1 Serving: Calories 330 (Calories from Fat 180); Fat 20g (Saturated 4g); Cholesterol 75mg; Sodium 330mg; Carbohydrate 10g (Dietary Fiber 3g); Protein 31g
*% **Daily Value:** Vitamin A 12%; Vitamin C 26%; Calcium 14%; Iron 14%*
***Diet Exchanges:** 4 Lean Meat, 2 Vegetable, 1 1/2 Fat*

Betty's Tip

Instead of making your own foil packets, try the new heavy-duty foil bags made especially for grilling.

Spicy Cajun
Grilled Chicken

PREP: 15 MIN ■ GRILL: 20 MIN ■ 8 SERVINGS

1/4 cup chili powder

2 tablespoons chopped fresh or 1 tablespoon dried oregano leaves

2 tablespoons chopped fresh or 1 tablespoon dried thyme leaves

1 tablespoon packed brown sugar

1 teaspoon pepper

1 teaspoon salt

8 boneless, skinless chicken breast halves (about 2 1/2 pounds)

3 medium tomatoes, chopped (2 1/4 cups)

1/2 cup whipping (heavy) cream

1 clove garlic, finely chopped

Brush grill rack with vegetable oil. Heat coals or gas grill for direct heat. Mix chili powder, oregano, thyme, brown sugar, pepper and salt; coat both sides of chicken with herb mixture.

Cover and grill chicken 4 to 5 inches from medium heat 15 to 20 minutes, turning once, until juice is no longer pink when centers of thickest pieces are cut.

Heat tomatoes, whipping cream and garlic in 1-quart saucepan over medium-high heat 2 minutes, stirring frequently. Top chicken with tomato mixture.

1 Serving: Calories 215 (Calories from Fat 80); Fat 9g (Saturated 4g); Cholesterol 90mg; Sodium 410mg; Carbohydrate 7g (Dietary Fiber 2g); Protein 28g
% Daily Value: Vitamin A 20%; Vitamin C 10%; Calcium 4%; Iron 10%
Diet Exchanges: 4 Lean Meat, 1 Vegetable, 1 Fat

Chicken with Peppers
and Artichokes

PREP: 20 MIN ▪ MARINATE: 8 HR ▪ GRILL: 20 MIN ▪ 4 SERVINGS

1 jar (6 ounces) marinated artichoke hearts

1/3 cup white wine or white wine vinegar

4 boneless, skinless chicken breast halves (about 1 1/4 pounds)

2 medium red bell peppers, each cut lengthwise into fourths

4 medium green onions, sliced (1/2 cup)

1/4 teaspoon pepper

Drain marinade from artichoke hearts; reserve. Mix reserved marinade and wine in shallow nonmetal dish or resealable plastic bag. Add chicken and bell peppers, turning to coat with marinade. Cover dish or seal bag and refrigerate at least 8 hours but no longer than 24 hours.

Heat coals or gas grill for direct heat. Remove chicken and bell peppers from marinade; reserve marinade. Cover and grill chicken 4 to 6 inches from medium heat 5 minutes. Turn chicken; add bell peppers to grill. Cover and grill 10 to 15 minutes longer or until bell peppers are tender and juice of chicken is no longer pink when centers of thickest pieces are cut.

Strain marinade. Mix marinade, artichoke hearts, onions and pepper. Heat to boiling; boil and stir 1 minute. Serve artichoke sauce with chicken and peppers.

1 Serving: Calories 185 (Calories from Fat 45); Fat 5g (Saturated 1g); Cholesterol 75mg; Sodium 200mg; Carbohydrate 10g (Dietary Fiber 4g); Protein 29g
% Daily Value: Vitamin A 36%; Vitamin C 100%; Calcium 4%; Iron 10%
Diet Exchanges: 4 Very Lean Meat, 2 Vegetable

Betty's Tip

The perfect make-ahead meal, these chicken breasts can marinate the night before. Add a purchased salad and a side of pasta and dinner is minutes away!

Caribbean Chicken
with Sweet Potatoes

PREP: 25 MIN ▪ CHILL AND MARINATE: 1 HR ▪ GRILL: 25 MIN

Tropical Fruit Salsa (below)

8 boneless, skinless chicken breast halves (about 2 1/2 pounds)

1 cup light rum or apple juice

1/4 cup honey

1 teaspoon ground allspice

1 teaspoon ground cinnamon

1 teaspoon ground ginger

1/2 teaspoon salt

2 cloves garlic, crushed

4 large sweet potatoes or yams, cut into 1/2-inch slices

Prepare Tropical Fruit Salsa. Place chicken in shallow glass or plastic dish. Mix remaining ingredients except sweet potatoes; pour over chicken. Cover and refrigerate 1 hour.

Brush grill rack with vegetable oil. Heat coals or gas grill for direct heat. Remove chicken from marinade; reserve marinade. Cover and grill chicken 4 to 5 inches from medium heat 10 minutes. Turn chicken; brush with marinade. Add sweet potato slices to grill. Cover and grill chicken and potato slices 10 to 15 minutes, brushing frequently with marinade, until chicken is no longer pink when centers of thickest pieces are cut. Discard any remaining marinade. Serve chicken and potato slices with salsa.

1 Serving: Calories 245 (Calories from Fat 35); Fat 4g (Saturated 1g); Cholesterol 75mg; Sodium 150mg; Carbohydrate 27g (Dietary Fiber 3g); Protein 28g
% Daily Value: Vitamin A 100%; Vitamin C 18%; Calcium 4%; Iron 8%
Diet Exchanges: 2 Starch, 3 Very Lean Meat

Tropical Fruit Salsa

1 mango

1 papaya

2 kiwifruit, peeled and chopped

1 jalapeño chili, seeded and finely chopped

1 cup pineapple chunks

1 tablespoon finely chopped red onion

1 tablespoon chopped fresh cilantro

2 tablespoons lime juice

Peel, pit and chop mango and papaya. Mix all ingredients in glass or plastic bowl. Cover and refrigerate 1 to 2 hours to blend flavors.

Betty's Tip

Sweet potatoes can have either a light or dark orange flesh. Their flavor is sweet and similar to winter squash.

Chili-Rubbed *Chicken*

PREP: 10 MIN ▪ MARINATE: 1 HR ▪ GRILL: 20 MIN ▪ 6 SERVINGS

6 boneless, skinless chicken breast halves (about 1 3/4 pounds)

3 tablespoons tomato paste

2 tablespoons chili powder

1 tablespoon white vinegar

1 teaspoon garlic salt

Two-Tomato Relish (below)

Place chicken in shallow glass or plastic dish. Mix tomato paste, chili powder, vinegar and garlic salt. Coat both sides of chicken with tomato paste mixture. Cover and refrigerate 1 hour. Prepare Two-Tomato Relish.

Brush grill rack with vegetable oil. Heat coals or gas grill for direct heat. Cover and grill chicken 4 to 5 inches from medium heat 15 to 20 minutes, turning once, until juice is no longer pink when centers of thickest pieces are cut. Serve with Two-Tomato Relish.

1 Serving: Calories 150 (Calories from Fat 35); Fat 4g (Saturated 1g); Cholesterol 75mg; Sodium 205mg; Carbohydrate 2g (Dietary Fiber 1g); Protein 27g
% Daily Value: Vitamin A 8%; Vitamin C 2%; Calcium 2%; Iron 6%
Diet Exchanges: 4 Very Lean Meat

Two-Tomato Relish

2 medium tomatoes, chopped (1 1/2 cups)

2 medium yellow tomatoes, chopped (1/2 cup)

1 tablespoon red wine vinegar

1 teaspoon chopped fresh or 1/4 teaspoon dried oregano leaves

Mix all ingredients. Cover and refrigerate until serving.

Betty's Tip

If you like hot and spicy foods, add crushed red pepper to the tomato paste mixture.

Blackberry-Glazed
Chicken

Prep: 5 min ▪ Grill: 25 min ▪ 6 servings

1/2 cup blackberry jam

1 tablespoon Dijon mustard

6 boneless, skinless chicken breast halves (about 1 3/4 pounds)

1 1/2 cups fresh or frozen (thawed, drained) blackberries

Brush grill rack with vegetable oil. Heat coals or gas grill for direct heat. Mix jam and mustard.

Cover and grill chicken 4 to 5 inches from medium heat 10 minutes. Turn chicken; brush with jam mixture. Cover and grill 10 to 15 minutes longer or until juice of chicken is no longer pink when centers of thickest pieces are cut. Serve chicken topped with blackberries.

1 Serving: Calories 225 (Calories from Fat 35); Fat 4g (Saturated 1g); Cholesterol 75mg; Sodium 110mg; Carbohydrate 22g (Dietary Fiber 2g); Protein 27g
% Daily Value: Vitamin A 0%; Vitamin C 8%; Calcium 2%; Iron 6%
Diet Exchanges: 1 Starch, 3 Very Lean Meat, 1/2 Fruit

Betty's Tip

Like a black raspberry, blackberries are large and sweet when ripe. Their color ranges from black to purplish black.

Chicken Breasts with
Tomato-Basil Butter

PREP: 10 MIN ▪ GRILL: 20 MIN ▪ 6 SERVINGS

6 boneless, skinless chicken breast halves (about 1 3/4 pounds)

2 teaspoons garlic pepper

1/2 cup margarine or butter, softened

1 tablespoon chopped fresh or 1 teaspoon dried basil leaves

3 tablespoons tomato paste

Brush grill rack with vegetable oil. Heat coals or gas grill for direct heat. Sprinkle chicken with garlic pepper.

Cover and grill chicken 4 to 5 inches from medium heat 15 to 20 minutes, turning once, until juice is no longer pink when centers of thickest pieces are cut. Mix remaining ingredients. Serve chicken topped with margarine mixture.

1 Serving: Calories 285 (Calories from Fat 170); Fat 19g (Saturated 11g); Cholesterol 115mg; Sodium 230mg; Carbohydrate 2g (Dietary Fiber 1g); Protein 27g
% Daily Value: Vitamin A 14%; Vitamin C 2%; Calcium 2%; Iron 6%
Diet Exchanges: 4 Lean Meat, 1 1/2 Fat

Betty's Tip

Here's a tip for no-waste tomato paste. If a recipe calls for a small amount of tomato paste, try using tomato paste that is available in a squeeze tube, which can be refrigerated after being opened. Or, place extra canned tomato paste in a plastic bag and store in the freezer.

Lemon Chicken with Grilled Fennel and Onions

PREP: 16 MIN ■ MARINATE: 30 MIN ■ GRILL: 20 MIN ■ 6 SERVINGS

6 bone-in chicken breast halves (about 3 pounds)

1/3 cup olive or vegetable oil

1 teaspoon grated lemon peel

1/4 cup lemon juice

2 tablespoons chopped fresh or 2 teaspoons dried oregano leaves

1/2 teaspoon salt

2 medium bulbs fennel, cut into 1/2-inch slices

1 medium red onion cut into 1/2-inch slices

1 small lemon, sliced

Oregano sprigs, if desired

Place chicken in shallow glass or plastic dish. Mix oil, lemon peel, lemon juice, chopped oregano and salt; pour over chicken. Cover and let stand 30 minutes.

Brush grill rack with vegetable oil. Heat coals or gas grill for direct heat. Remove chicken from marinade. Brush fennel and onion with marinade. Cover and grill chicken (skin sides down), fennel and onion 4 to 5 inches from medium heat 15 to 20 minutes, turning once and brushing frequently with marinade, until juice of chicken is no longer pink when centers of thickest pieces are cut. Discard any remaining marinade. Serve chicken with lemon slices. Garnish with oregano sprigs.

1 Serving: Calories 285 (Calories from Fat 155); Fat 17g (Saturated 3g); Cholesterol 75mg; Sodium 230mg; Carbohydrate 8g (Dietary Fiber 3g); Protein 28g
% Daily Value: Vitamin A 2%; Vitamin C 10%; Calcium 6%; Iron 8%
Diet Exchanges: 4 Lean Meat, 1 Vegetable, 1 Fat

Betty's Tip

For easy entertaining, serve this lemony chicken with fresh tomato slices and angel hair pasta.

Maple- and Cranberry-Glazed Chicken

PREP: 5 MIN ▪ GRILL: 20 MIN ▪ 6 SERVINGS

1 can (16 ounces) whole berry cranberry sauce

1/2 cup maple-flavored syrup

1/2 teaspoon salt

6 boneless, skinless chicken breast halves (about 1 3/4 pounds)

Brush grill rack with vegetable oil. Heat coals or gas grill for direct heat. Mix half of the cranberry sauce with the syrup. Sprinkle salt over chicken.

Cover and grill chicken 4 to 5 inches from medium heat 10 minutes; turn chicken. Grill 10 to 15 minutes longer, brushing occasionally with cranberry mixture, until juice of chicken is no longer pink when centers of thickest pieces are cut. Serve with remaining cranberry sauce.

1 Serving: Calories 365 (Calories from Fat 65); Fat 7g (Saturated 2g); Cholesterol 75mg; Sodium 310mg; Carbohydrate 49g (Dietary Fiber 1g); Protein 27g
% Daily Value: Vitamin A 2%; Vitamin C 0%; Calcium 2%; Iron 6%
Diet Exchanges: 2 Starch, 3 Lean Meat, 1 Fruit

Betty's Tip

For an autumn treat, try serving this chicken with sage dressing and roasted root vegetables, such as carrots, onions, parsnips and rutabagas.

Spinach Salad with *Grilled Chicken and Raspberries*

PREP: 18 MIN ▪ GRILL: 20 MIN ▪ 4 SERVINGS

4 boneless, skinless chicken breast halves (about 1 1/4 pounds)

3/4 cup raspberry or regular vinaigrette dressing

6 cups bite-size pieces spinach or lettuce

1 pint (2 cups) raspberries

1 mango, peeled and sliced

Brush grill rack with vegetable oil. Heat coals or gas grill for direct heat. Brush chicken with 2 tablespoons of the dressing. Cover and grill chicken 4 to 5 inches from medium heat 15 to 20 minutes, turning once and brushing with 2 tablespoons dressing, until juice of chicken is no longer pink when centers of thickest pieces are cut.

Divide spinach among 4 plates. Top with raspberries and mango. Cut chicken diagonally into 1/2-inch slices; place on salads. Drizzle with remaining dressing.

1 Serving: *Calories 225 (Calories from Fat 45); Fat 5g (Saturated 1g); Cholesterol 75mg; Sodium 430mg; Carbohydrate 22g (Dietary Fiber 6g); Protein 29g*
% Daily Value: *Vitamin A 58%; Vitamin C 70%; Calcium 8%; Iron 14%*
Diet Exchanges: *3 1/2 Very Lean Meat, 2 Vegetable, 1 Fruit*

Try This

For an interesting color combination, use golden raspberries. Golden raspberries are not as tart as red raspberries and have a hint of strawberry flavor

Chicken Salad with *Grilled Pineapple*

PREP: 16 MIN ▪ GRILL: 20 MIN ▪ 6 SERVINGS

Mango Vinaigrette (below)

1 small pineapple, peeled and cut into 1/2-inch slices

6 boneless, skinless chicken breast halves (about 1 3/4 pounds)

1/4 cup packed brown sugar

6 cups bite-size pieces romaine

3/4 cup pecan halves, toasted (page 179)

Prepare Mango Vinaigrette. Cut each pineapple slice in half. Brush grill rack with vegetable oil. Heat coals or gas grill for direct heat. Brush chicken with 1/4 cup of the Mango Vinaigrette.

Cover and grill chicken 4 to 5 inches from medium heat 15 to 20 minutes, turning once, until juice of chicken is no longer pink when centers of thickest pieces are cut. Coat pineapple with brown sugar. Add pineapple for last 2 to 4 minutes of grilling, turning once, until golden brown.

Place romaine on large platter; top with pineapple. Cut chicken diagonally into 1/2-inch slices; arrange around romaine. Sprinkle pecans over salad. Drizzle with remaining vinaigrette.

1 Serving: Calories 490 (Calories from Fat 280); Fat 31g (Saturated 4g); Cholesterol 75mg; Sodium 170mg; Carbohydrate 27g (Dietary Fiber 3g); Protein 29g
% Daily Value: Vitamin A 22%; Vitamin C 46%; Calcium 4%; Iron 12%
Diet Exchanges: 3 1/2 Lean Meat, 2 Vegetable, 1 Fruit, 4 Fat

Mango Vinaigrette

1 large mango, peeled and pitted

1/2 cup light olive oil

2 tablespoons cider vinegar

1 teaspoon sugar

1/4 teaspoon salt

Mash mango. Mix mango and remaining ingredients.

Try This

If available, use bottled mango vinaigrette marinade to brush on chicken and use as a dressing.

Autumn Grilled
Chicken

PREP: 12 MIN ■ GRILL: 15 MIN ■ 4 SERVINGS

1 pound cut-up boneless chicken breast for stir-fry

2 large firm ripe pears, sliced

1 large cooking apple, sliced

1/2 cup roasted-apple vinaigrette or malt vinegar

2 tablespoons chopped fresh or 1 teaspoon dried sage leaves

1/2 teaspoon salt

Heat coals or gas grill for direct heat. Place chicken, pears and apple on one side of each of 4 sheets of heavy-duty aluminum foil, 18 × 12 inches. Top with vinaigrette, sage and salt. Fold other half of foil over chicken and fruit so edges meet. Seal edges, making a tight 1/2-inch fold; fold again. Allow space on sides for circulation and expansion. Repeat folding to seal each side.

Cover and grill packets 4 to 5 inches from medium heat 10 to 15 minutes or until chicken is no longer pink in center. Place foil packets on plates. To serve, cut a large **X** across top of packet; fold back foil.

1 Serving: Calories 220 (Calories from Fat 35); Fat 4g (Saturated 1g); Cholesterol 70mg; Sodium 260mg; Carbohydrate 25g (Dietary Fiber 4g); Protein 25g
*% **Daily Value**: Vitamin A 0%; Vitamin C 6%; Calcium 2%; Iron 8%*
Diet Exchanges: 3 1/2 Very Lean Meat, 1 1/2 Fruit

Try This

Roasted-apple marinade is a bottled fat-free dressing and marinade made from fresh apples that have been roasted and mixed with champagne vinegar, sugar and spices. It is deep brown in color with a toasty, savory apple flavor. Look for it along with the salad dressings or marinades in your grocery store.

Betty's Tip

Sage has a pungent, musty flavor that pairs well with apples and chicken.

Chicken and Summer
Fruit Kabobs

PREP: 12 MIN ▪ GRILL: 20 MIN ▪ 6 SERVINGS

1 pound boneless, skinless chicken breasts, cut into 1 1/2-inch pieces

2 medium peaches or nectarines, cut into 1-inch wedges

2 medium red plums, cut into 1-inch wedges

1 medium purple plum, cut into 1-inch wedges

1/2 cup peach or apricot jam

1/2 teaspoon salt

Brush grill rack with vegetable oil. Heat coals or gas grill for direct heat. Thread chicken, peaches and plums alternately on each of six 10- to 12-inch metal skewers, leaving space between each piece. Mix jam and salt.

Cover and grill kabobs 4 to 5 inches from medium heat 15 to 20 minutes, turning occasionally and brushing with jam, until chicken is no longer pink in center.

1 Serving: Calories 190 (Calories from Fat 25); Fat 3g (Saturated 1g); Cholesterol 45mg; Sodium 250mg; Carbohydrate 25g (Dietary Fiber 1g); Protein 17g
% Daily Value: Vitamin A 2%; Vitamin C 6%; Calcium 2%; Iron 4%
Diet Exchanges: 2 Lean Meat, 1 1/2 Fruit

Betty's Tip

Dress up these kabobs for entertaining by serving them on rice pilaf or cooked wild rice.

Grilled Texas Turkey *Burgers*

PREP: 10 MIN ▪ GRILL: 16 MIN ▪ 4 SERVINGS

1 pound ground turkey

1/3 cup barbecue sauce

1 can (4 ounces) chopped green chilies, drained

4 slices (1 ounce each) Monterey Jack cheese with jalapeño peppers

4 hamburger buns, split

Brush grill rack with vegetable oil. Heat coals or gas grill for direct heat. Mix turkey, barbecue sauce and chilies. Shape mixture into 4 patties, each about 3/4 inch thick.

Cover and grill patties 4 to 6 inches from medium heat 14 to 16 minutes, turning once, until no longer pink in center. About 1 minute before burgers are done, top each with cheese slice. Grill until cheese is melted. Serve on buns.

1 Serving: Calories 390 (Calories from Fat 153); Fat 17g (Saturated 8g); Cholesterol 100mg; Sodium 720mg; Carbohydrate 26g (Dietary Fiber 2g); Protein 36g
*% **Daily Value:** Vitamin A 14%; Vitamin C 16%; Calcium 28%; Iron 16%*
Diet Exchanges: 1 Starch, 4 Lean Meat, 2 Vegetable, 1 Fat

Turkey-Cheddar *Burgers*

PREP: 15 MIN ▪ GRILL: 21 MIN ▪ 4 SERVINGS

1 pound ground turkey

1/2 cup shredded Cheddar cheese (2 ounces)

1 small onion, finely chopped (1/4 cup)

1 tablespoon Worcestershire sauce

1/2 teaspoon salt

4 slices (1 ounce each) Cheddar cheese

4 English muffins, split and toasted

Brush grill rack with vegetable oil. Heat coals or gas grill for direct heat. Mix turkey, shredded cheese, onion, Worcestershire sauce and salt. Shape mixture into 4 patties, about 3/4 inch thick.

Cover and grill patties 4 to 5 inches from medium heat 15 to 20 minutes, turning once, until no longer pink. Top burgers with sliced cheese. Grill 1 minute to melt cheese. Serve burgers on English muffins.

1 Serving: Calories 455 (Calories from Fat 190); Fat 21g (Saturated 10g); Cholesterol 120mg; Sodium 730mg; Carbohydrate 28g (Dietary Fiber 2g); Protein 40g
% Daily Value: Vitamin A 10%; Vitamin C 0%; Calcium 34%; Iron 16%
Diet Exchanges: 2 Starch, 5 Lean Meat, 1 Fat

Try This

Mix smoked Cheddar
cheese into the ground
turkey mixture for
Smoked Cheddar-Turkey
Burgers.

Blue Cheese
Burgers

Prep: 10 min ▪ Grill: 20 min ▪ 4 servings

1 pound ground turkey

1/4 cup mayonnaise or salad dressing

4 ounces crumbled blue cheese

4 onion or plain hamburger buns, split

1 medium red onion sliced, if desired

Brush grill rack with vegetable oil. Heat coals or gas grill for direct heat. Mix turkey, mayonnaise and blue cheese. Shape mixture into 4 patties, about 3/4 inch thick.

Cover and grill patties 4 to 5 inches from medium heat 15 to 20 minutes, turning once, until turkey is no longer pink in center. Serve burgers on buns with onion slices.

1 Serving: Calories 485 (Calories from Fat 250); Fat 28g (Saturated 9g); Cholesterol 105mg; Sodium 790mg; Carbohydrate 25g (Dietary Fiber 2g); Protein 35g
% Daily Value: Vitamin A 8%; Vitamin C 0%; Calcium 22%; Iron 14%
Diet Exchanges: 1 Starch, 4 Lean Meat, 2 Vegetable, 3 Fat

Betty's Tip

Attention, blue cheese lovers! These burgers stay very moist and flavorful. Try topping them with crisp cooked bacon.

Italian *Burgers*

PREP: 10 MIN ▪ GRILL: 16 MIN ▪ 4 SERVINGS

1 pound ground turkey

1/3 cup spaghetti sauce

3 tablespoons finely chopped onion

4 slices (1 ounce each) provolone cheese

8 slices Italian bread, grilled, if desired

Sliced tomato, if desired

Sliced olives, if desired

Brush grill rack with vegetable oil. Heat coals or gas grill for direct heat. Mix turkey, spaghetti sauce and onion. Shape mixture into 4 patties, each about 3/4 inch thick.

Cover and grill patties 4 to 6 inches from medium heat 14 to 16 minutes, turning once, until no longer pink in center. About 1 minute before burgers are done, top each with cheese slice. Grill until cheese is melted. Serve between bread slices with tomatoes and olives.

1 Serving: Calories 380 (Calories from Fat 145); Fat 16g (Saturated 7g); Cholesterol 100mg; Sodium 680mg; Carbohydrate 25g (Dietary Fiber 2g); Protein 36g
% Daily Value: Vitamin A 10%; Vitamin C 2%; Calcium 26%; Iron 14%
Diet Exchanges: 1 Starch, 4 Lean Meat, 2 Vegetable, 1 Fat

Betty's Tip

Use crumpled aluminum foil to scrape cooked-on food bits from the grill rack. This is a great way to recycle slightly used foil!

Firecracker Chicken Wings

PREP: 10 MIN ▪ MARINATE: 1 HR ▪ GRILL: 25 MIN ▪ 4 SERVINGS

12 chicken wings (2 1/2 pounds)

2 tablespoons chili powder

1 1/2 teaspoons dried oregano leaves

1 1/4 teaspoons ground red pepper (cayenne)

1 teaspoon garlic salt

1 teaspoon ground cumin

1 teaspoon pepper

Sour cream, if desired

Fold wing tips under opposite ends to form triangles.

Place remaining ingredients except sour cream in resealable plastic bag. Seal bag and shake to blend seasonings. Add chicken. Seal bag and shake until chicken is coated with seasonings. Refrigerate at least 1 hour but no longer than 24 hours.

Heat coals or gas grill for direct heat. Cover and grill chicken 4 to 6 inches from medium heat 20 to 25 minutes, turning after 10 minutes, until juice of chicken is no longer pink when centers of thickest pieces are cut. Serve chicken with sour cream.

1 Serving: Calories 305 (Calories from Fat 190); Fat 21g (Saturated 6g); Cholesterol 85mg; Sodium 360mg; Carbohydrate 3g (Dietary Fiber 2g); Protein 28g
% Daily Value: Vitamin A 20%; Vitamin C 2%; Calcium 4%; Iron 14%
Diet Exchanges: 4 Medium-Fat Meat

Betty's Tip

You can serve these spicy wings as appetizers, too. The sour cream cools the heat, or try them with a bowl of chilled blue cheese dip.

Chapter 6

Salads, Sandwiches and Pizza

Quick Chicken Caesar Salad

PREP: 10 MIN ▪ 6 SERVINGS

3 cups cut-up cooked chicken

1 large or 2 small bunches romaine, torn into bite-size pieces (10 cups)

1 1/2 cups Caesar or garlic-flavored croutons

1/3 cup freshly grated Parmesan cheese

Freshly ground pepper

2/3 cup Caesar dressing

Place chicken, romaine, croutons, cheese and pepper in large bowl. Toss with dressing until coated.

1 Serving: Calories 295 (Calories from Fat 160); Fat 18g (Saturated 4g); Cholesterol 70mg; Sodium 540mg; Carbohydrate 10g (Dietary Fiber 1g); Protein 24g
% Daily Value: Vitamin A 14%; Vitamin C 20%; Calcium 10%; Iron 10%
Diet Exchanges: 3 Medium-Fat Meat, 2 Vegetable, 1/2 Fat

Betty's Tip

Check out the freezer case for cooked chicken. You should be able to find seasoned and unseasoned varieties of cubed cooked chicken and grilled boneless, skinless chicken breasts to make putting together this tasty salad a snap.

Caribbean Chicken
and Black Bean Salad

PREP: 20 MIN ▪ 4 SERVINGS

Spicy Lime Dressing (below)

2 cups cut-up cooked chicken

1/4 cup chopped fresh cilantro

1 large tomato, chopped (1 cup)

1 medium avocado, chopped

1 small yellow summer squash, chopped

1 can (15 ounces) black beans, rinsed and drained

Leaf lettuce

Prepare Spicy Lime Dressing. Toss remaining ingredients except lettuce in large bowl. Pour dressing over salad; toss. Serve on lettuce.

1 Serving: Calories 445 (Calories from Fat 205); Fat 23g (Saturated 5g); Cholesterol 60mg; Sodium 630mg; Carbohydrate 40g (Dietary Fiber 10g); Protein 29g
% Daily Value: Vitamin A 10%; Vitamin C 32%; Calcium 10%; Iron 24%
Diet Exchanges: 2 Starch, 2 1/2 Medium-Fat Meat, 2 Vegetable, 1 Fat

Spicy Lime Dressing

1/4 cup lime juice

2 tablespoons olive or vegetable oil

1 tablespoon honey

1/2 teaspoon chili powder

1/4 teaspoon ground cumin

1/4 teaspoon salt

2 or 3 drops red pepper sauce

Shake all ingredients in tightly covered container.

Betty's Tip

You'll get the most juice from a lime or lemon if you roll it on the counter or microwave on High 10 seconds before cutting.

Fruited Taco *Salad*

PREP: 15 MIN ▪ 4 SERVINGS

Lime Cumin Vinaigrette (below)

6 cups bite-size pieces salad greens

2 cups coarsely shredded cooked chicken

1/2 cup julienne strips peeled jicama

1 medium mango, seeded and cut up

1 cup raspberries

Lime wedges, if desired

Tortilla chips, if desired

Prepare Lime Cumin Vinaigrette. Toss salad greens, chicken, jicama, mango, raspberries and vinaigrette. Just before serving, lightly squeeze juice from lime wedges over salad. Serve with tortilla chips.

1 Serving: Calories 390 (Calories from Fat 215); Fat 24g (Saturated 4g); Cholesterol 60mg; Sodium 240mg; Carbohydrate 28g (Dietary Fiber 5g); Protein 21g
% Daily Value: Vitamin A 30%; Vitamin C 100%; Calcium 6%; Iron 12%
Diet Exchanges: 3 Medium-Fat Meat, 2 Fruit, 1 Fat

Lime Cumin Vinaigrette

1/4 cup olive or vegetable oil

3 tablespoons lime juice

1 tablespoon honey

1 1/2 tablespoons chopped fresh cilantro

3/4 teaspoon ground cumin

1/4 teaspoon salt

1/8 teaspoon pepper

1 to 2 cloves garlic, finely chopped

Shake all ingredients in tightly covered container.

Betty's Tip

Jicama is a large root vegetable with a thin brown skin and a crisp white flesh. This sweet, nutty vegetable is delicious raw or cooked. Be sure to peel the skin before using.

Fresh Berry-Chicken *Salad*

PREP: 10 MIN ■ COOK: 22 MIN ■ CHILL: 1 HR ■ 4 SERVINGS

4 boneless, skinless chicken breast halves (about 1 1/4 pounds)

2 1/2 cups chicken broth

2 tablespoons raspberry vinegar

1 bag (10 ounces) salad mix

1/2 pint (1 cup) raspberries

1/2 pint (1 cup) strawberries, cut in half

Raspberry Vinaigrette (below)

Place chicken, broth and vinegar in 12-inch skillet. Heat to boiling; reduce heat. Cover and simmer 15 to 20 minutes or until juice of chicken is no longer pink when centers of thickest pieces are cut. Refrigerate chicken in broth about 1 hour or until cool.

Remove chicken from broth; discard broth. Cut chicken diagonally into 1/4-inch slices. Arrange chicken on salad mix. Top with berries. Drizzle Raspberry Vinaigrette over salad.

1 Serving: Calories 410 (Calories from Fat 215); Fat 24g (Saturated 4g); Cholesterol 85mg; Sodium 740mg; Carbohydrate 16g (Dietary Fiber 4g); Protein 35g
% Daily Value: Vitamin A 20%; Vitamin C 78%; Calcium 6%; Iron 14%
Diet Exchanges: 5 Lean Meat, 1 Fruit, 2 Fat

Raspberry Vinaigrette

1/3 cup vegetable oil

2 tablespoons raspberry vinegar

2 tablespoons raspberry jam

Beat all ingredients, using wire whisk.

Betty's Tip

Don't have an hour to spare to chill the chicken? Serve the salad warm; it's just as delicious.

Thai Chicken
Salad

PREP: 16 MIN ■ 4 SERVINGS

Honey-Ginger Dressing (below)

6 cups bite-size pieces assorted salad greens

1 1/2 cups shredded cooked chicken

1 medium carrot, shredded (3/4 cup)

1 can (14 to 15 ounces) baby corn nuggets, drained

1/3 cup flaked coconut, toasted*

Prepare Honey-Ginger Dressing. Place salad greens, chicken, carrot and corn in large bowl. Pour dressing over salad; toss until coated. Sprinkle with coconut.

1 Serving: Calories 375 (Calories from Fat 190); Fat 21g (Saturated 5g); Cholesterol 45mg; Sodium 750mg; Carbohydrate 32g (Dietary Fiber 4g); Protein 19g
*% **Daily Value:*** Vitamin A 32%; Vitamin C 26%; Calcium 4%; Iron 14%
Diet Exchanges: 1 Starch, 1 1/2 Lean Meat, 3 Vegetable, 3 Fat

*To toast coconut, cook in ungreased heavy skillet over medium-low heat 6 to 14 minutes, stirring frequently until browning begins, then stirring constantly until golden brown. Or bake uncovered in ungreased shallow pan in 350° oven 5 to 7 minutes, stirring occasionally, until golden brown.

Honey-Ginger Dressing

1/4 cup vegetable oil

2 tablespoons balsamic or cider vinegar

2 tablespoons soy sauce

1 tablespoon honey

1 teaspoon grated gingerroot

Shake all ingredients in tightly covered container.

Betty's Tip

Go ahead and use pack-
aged, assorted prewashed
salad greens for this
recipe to save time.

Chopped Asian *Salad*

PREP: 25 MIN ■ 4 SERVINGS

Lime Dressing (below)

2 cups chopped escarole

I cup chopped cooked chicken

I small jicama, peeled and chopped (I cup)

I large papaya, peeled and chopped (I cup)

I large yellow or red bell pepper, chopped (I cup)

1/2 cup dry-roasted peanuts

1/4 cup chopped cilantro

Prepare Lime Dressing. Place remaining ingredients except peanuts and cilantro in large bowl. Pour dressing over salad; toss until coated. Top with peanuts and cilantro.

1 Serving: Calories 425 (Calories from Fat 252); Fat 28g (Saturated 5g); Cholesterol 30mg; Sodium 260mg; Carbohydrate 36g (Dietary Fiber 9g); Protein 16g
% Daily Value: Vitamin A 10%; Vitamin C 100%; Calcium 6%; Iron 10%
Diet Exchanges: 2 Starch, 1 High-Fat Meat, 1 Vegetable, 3 Fat

Lime Dressing

1/3 cup frozen (thawed) limeade

1/4 cup vegetable oil

I tablespoon rice or white vinegar

I teaspoon grated gingerroot

1/4 teaspoon salt

Shake all ingredients in tightly covered container.

Betty's Tip

A food processor makes quick work of the chopping for this salad. Chop the vegetables in advance, and store in plastic bags.

Chicken-Curry-Couscous Salad

PREP: 22 MIN ■ CHILL: 1 HR ■ 4 SERVINGS

Curry Dressing (below)

2 cups cooked couscous

I cup diced cooked chicken

I cup raisins

I medium red or yellow bell pepper, cut into thin strips

6 medium green onions, chopped (6 tablespoons)

I can (15 to 16 ounces) garbanzo beans, rinsed and drained

1/2 cup chopped roasted almonds

Prepare Curry Dressing. Place remaining ingredients except almonds in large bowl. Pour dressing over salad; toss until coated. Cover and refrigerate about 1 hour or until chilled. Top with almonds.

1 Serving: Calories 710 (Calories from Fat 295); Fat 33g (Saturated 4g); Cholesterol 30mg; Sodium 540mg; Carbohydrate 89g (Dietary Fiber 14g); Protein 28g
% Daily Value: Vitamin A 18%; Vitamin C 100%; Calcium 14%; Iron 34%
Diet Exchanges: 5 Starch, 1 Lean Meat, 2 Vegetable, 6 Fat

Curry Dressing

1/3 cup light olive or vegetable oil

I tablespoon lemon juice

I teaspoon sugar

1/2 teaspoon curry powder

1/4 teaspoon salt

1/8 teaspoon ground allspice

Shake all ingredients in tightly covered container.

Betty's Tip

Create a Middle Eastern luncheon by serving this salad with flatbread or pita breads.

Wild Rice-Chicken Salad
with Raspberry Vinaigrette

PREP: 10 MIN ▪ CHILL: 1 HR ▪ 6 SERVINGS

3 cups cold cooked wild rice

1 1/2 cups cubed cooked chicken or turkey

4 medium green onions, chopped (1/4 cup)

1 medium green bell pepper, chopped (1 cup)

1 can (8 ounces) sliced water chestnuts, drained

1 package (6 ounces) diced dried fruits and raisins

1/3 cup raspberry vinegar

1/4 cup honey

2 tablespoons vegetable oil

Mix all ingredients except vinegar, honey and oil in large bowl. Shake vinegar, honey and oil in tightly covered container. Pour over wild rice mixture; toss. Cover and refrigerate 1 to 2 hours to blend flavors.

1 Serving: Calories 330 (Calories from Fat 70); Fat 8g (Saturated 1g); Cholesterol 30mg; Sodium 45mg; Carbohydrate 55g (Dietary Fiber 5g); Protein 14g
% Daily Value: Vitamin A 8%; Vitamin C 38%; Calcium 4%; Iron 12%
Diet Exchanges: 2 Starch, 1 Lean Meat, 2 Vegetable, 1 Fruit

Try This

Instead of diced dried fruits and raisins, try dried cherries or cranberries.

Greek Orzo
Salad

PREP: 20 MIN ▪ 4 SERVINGS

4 cups cooked rosamarina (orzo) pasta

1 cup shredded cooked chicken

2 medium cucumbers, chopped (1 1/2 cups)

1 medium red or green bell pepper, chopped (1 cup)

1/3 cup balsamic vinaigrette

1/2 cup pitted Kalamata or Greek olives

1/4 cup crumbled feta cheese

Place pasta, chicken, cucumbers and bell pepper in large bowl. Pour vinaigrette over salad; toss until coated. Top with olives and cheese.

1 Serving: Calories 305 (Calories from Fat 65); Fat 7g (Saturated 2g); Cholesterol 40mg; Sodium 280mg; Carbohydrate 46g (Dietary Fiber 4g); Protein 19g
% Daily Value: Vitamin A 20%; Vitamin C 100%; Calcium 8%; Iron 18%
Diet Exchanges: 2 Starch, 1 Lean Meat, 3 Vegetable, 1 Fat

Betty's Tip

Kalamata olives, grown in the Mediterranean, are sun ripened, cured and pickled in brine. Available both pitted and unpitted, they have a salty, mild wine flavor and a texture that is soft and creamy.

Italian Chopped
Salad

PREP: 23 MIN ▪ 4 SERVINGS

Basil Vinaigrette (below)

6 cups chopped romaine

I cup fresh basil leaves

I cup cut-up cooked chicken

2 large tomatoes, chopped (2 cups)

2 medium cucumbers, chopped (I 1/2 cups)

I package (3 ounces) Italian salami, chopped

I can (15 to 16 ounces) cannellini beans, rinsed and drained

Prepare Basil Vinaigrette. Place remaining ingredients in large bowl. Pour vinaigrette over salad; toss until coated.

1 Serving: Calories 480 (Calories from Fat 260); Fat 29g (Saturated 6g); Cholesterol 45mg; Sodium 590mg; Carbohydrate 38g (Dietary Fiber 10g); Protein 27g
% Daily Value: Vitamin A 24%; Vitamin C 58%; Calcium 16%; Iron 34%
Diet Exchanges: 2 Starch, 2 Lean Meat, 2 Vegetable, 4 Fat

Basil Vinaigrette

1/3 cup vegetable oil

1/4 cup red wine vinegar

2 tablespoons chopped fresh or 2 teaspoons dried basil leaves

I teaspoon sugar

1/4 teaspoon salt

Shake all ingredients in tightly covered container.

Sausalito Chicken and *Seafood Salad*

PREP: 18 MIN ▪ 4 SERVINGS

6 cups bite-size pieces assorted salad greens

1 cup diced cooked chicken

1 large avocado, sliced

1 package (8 ounces) refrigerated imitation crabmeat chunks

1 can (4 ounces) whole green chilies, drained and sliced lengthwise

1 container (6 ounces) frozen guacamole, thawed

1/2 cup sour cream

1 large tomato, chopped (1 cup)

Lime or lemon wedges

Divide salad greens among 4 plates. Top with chicken, avocado, crabmeat and chilies. Mix guacamole and sour cream; spoon over salad. Top with tomato. Garnish with lime wedges.

1 Serving: Calories 265 (Calories from Fat 125); Fat 14g (Saturated 3g); Cholesterol 50mg; Sodium 750mg; Carbohydrate 17g (Dietary Fiber 5g); Protein 23g
% Daily Value: Vitamin A 22%; Vitamin C 82%; Calcium 10%; Iron 12%
Diet Exchanges: 3 Lean Meat, 3 Vegetable, 1 Fat

Betty's Tip

Sausalito is a quaint town across the bay from San Francisco that's known for its outdoor cafes and wonderful seafood. Our salad will transport you there!

Honey-Mustard
Chicken Sandwiches

PREP: 10 MIN ▪ GRILL: 20 MIN ▪ 4 SANDWICHES

1/4 cup Dijon mustard

2 tablespoons honey

1 teaspoon dried oregano leaves

1/8 to 1/4 teaspoon ground red pepper (cayenne)

4 boneless, skinless chicken breast halves (about 1 1/4 pounds)

4 whole-grain sandwich buns, split

4 slices tomato

Leaf lettuce

Heat coals or gas grill for direct heat.

Mix mustard, honey, oregano and red pepper. Brush on chicken. Cover and grill chicken 4 to 6 inches from medium heat 15 to 20 minutes, brushing frequently with mustard mixture and turning occasionally, until juice of chicken is no longer pink when centers of thickest pieces are cut. Discard any remaining mustard mixture.

Serve chicken on buns with tomato and lettuce.

*1 **Sandwich:** Calories 275 (Calories from Fat 55); Fat 6g (Saturated 1g); Cholesterol 75mg; Sodium 450mg; Carbohydrate 27g (Dietary Fiber 3g); Protein 31g*
*% **Daily Value:** Vitamin A 6%; Vitamin C 12%; Calcium 6%; Iron 14%*
__Diet Exchanges:__ 1 Starch, 3 1/2 Lean Meat, 2 Vegetable

Betty's Tip

These sandwiches can be broiled on rainy days or when you don't feel like firing up the grill. Place the chicken on the rack of the broiler pan and brush with mustard mixture. Broil 4 to 6 inches from heat for 15 to 20 minutes turning once and brushing with additional mustard mixture.

Montana
Panini

PREP: 8 MIN COOK: 5 MIN ▪ 6 SANDWICHES

**12 slices sourdough bread,
1/2 inch thick**

**3 tablespoons margarine or
butter, softened**

**3/4 pound thinly sliced
cooked deli turkey**

**12 slices turkey bacon,
crisply cooked, broken in half**

1 large tomato, sliced

**6 slices (1 ounce each)
Colby-Monterey Jack cheese**

**Avocado Ranch Dressing
(below)**

Spread one side of each bread slice with margarine. Place 6 bread slices margarine sides down; top with turkey, bacon, tomato, cheese and dressing. Top with remaining bread slices, margarine sides up.

Cover and cook sandwiches in 12-inch skillet over medium heat 4 to 5 minutes, turning once, until bread is crisp and cheese is melted.

1 Serving: Calories 515 (Calories from Fat 300); Fat 33g (Saturated 10g); Cholesterol 75mg; Sodium 1680mg; Carbohydrate 31g (Dietary Fiber 3g); Protein 27g
% Daily Value: Vitamin A 20%; Vitamin C 14%; Calcium 22%; Iron 14%
Diet Exchanges: 2 Starch, 3 Lean Meat, 4 Fat

Avocado Ranch Dressing

1/4 cup ranch dressing

1 small avocado, mashed

Mix ingredients.

Jerk Turkey *Panini*

PREP: 8 MIN COOK: 5 MIN ▪ 4 SANDWICHES

8 slices crusty bread, 1/2 inch thick

2 tablespoons margarine or butter, softened

1/2 pound thinly sliced cooked deli turkey

1 medium papaya, peeled, pitted and sliced

4 slices (1 ounce each) Monterey Jack cheese with jalapeño peppers

1/4 cup jerk seasoning sauce or fruit chutney

Spread one side of each bread slice with margarine. Place 4 bread slices margarine sides down; top with turkey, papaya and cheese. Top with remaining bread slices, margarine sides up.

Cover and cook sandwiches in 12-inch skillet over medium heat 4 to 5 minutes, turning once, until bread is crisp and cheese is melted. Serve with sauce.

1 Serving: Calories 480 (Calories from Fat 170); Fat 19g (Saturated 8g); Cholesterol 55mg; Sodium 1390mg; Carbohydrate 56g (Dietary Fiber 3g); Protein 24g
% Daily Value: Vitamin A 20%; Vitamin C 40%; Calcium 32%; Iron 18%
Diet Exchanges: 3 Starch, 1 1/2 Lean Meat, 2 Vegetable, 3 Fat

Try This

Can't find ripe papaya? No worries! Slices of fresh pineapple or peaches taste great, too!

Chicken BLT
Sandwiches

PREP: 10 MIN ■ COOK: 20 MIN ■ 4 SANDWICHES

2 teaspoons vegetable oil

4 boneless, skinless chicken breast halves (about 1 1/4 pounds)

1/4 cup Thousand Island dressing

4 whole wheat sandwich buns, split

4 lettuce leaves

8 slices tomato

4 slices bacon, cooked, drained and broken in half

Heat oil in 10-inch skillet over medium-high heat. Cook chicken in oil 15 to 20 minutes, turning once, until juice is no longer pink when centers of thickest pieces are cut.

Spread dressing on cut sides of buns. Layer chicken, lettuce, tomato and bacon on bottoms of buns. Top with tops of buns.

1 Serving: Calories 380 (Calories from Fat 155); Fat 16g (Saturated 4g); Cholesterol 95mg; Sodium 550mg; Carbohydrate 23g (Dietary Fiber 4g); Protein 37g
*% **Daily Value:** Vitamin A 4%; Vitamin C 12%; Calcium 4%; Iron 16%*
***Diet Exchanges:** 1 Starch, 4 Lean Meat, 2 Vegetable, 1 Fat*

Betty's Tip

To reduce the fat in this recipe, omit the oil and spray a nonstick skillet with cooking spray, use reduced-fat or fat-free salad dressing, use reduced-calorie and reduced-fat buns (often labeled "light") and turkey bacon.

Chicken-Pesto
Sandwiches

PREP: 10 MIN ▪ BROIL: 20 MIN ▪ 6 SANDWICHES

6 boneless, skinless chicken breast halves (about 1 3/4 pounds)

1/2 teaspoon salt

2 tablespoons chopped fresh or 2 teaspoons dried oregano leaves

1 round focaccia bread (about 10 inches in diameter)

1 container (7 ounces) refrigerated pesto

6 slices tomato

1 1/2 cups shredded spinach

Flatten each chicken breast half to 1/4-inch thickness between sheets of plastic wrap or waxed paper. Sprinkle with salt and oregano.

Set oven control to broil. Place chicken on rack in broiler pan. Broil with tops 4 to 6 inches from heat 15 to 20 minutes, turning once, until juice is no longer pink when centers of thickest pieces are cut.

Cut focaccia horizontally in half; cut into 6 wedges. Spread pesto on cut sides of bread. Layer chicken, tomato and spinach on bottom wedges. Top with top wedges.

1 Serving: Calories 530 (Calories from Fat 250); Fat 28g (Saturated 5g); Cholesterol 85mg; Sodium 1090mg; Carbohydrate 34g (Dietary Fiber 3g); Protein 38g
% Daily Value: Vitamin A 10%; Vitamin C 12%; Calcium 14%; Iron 24%
Diet Exchanges: 2 Starch, 4 Lean Meat, 1 Vegetable, 3 Fat

Betty's Tip

To speed up the preparation of this recipe, look for prewashed spinach.

Chicken Quesadilla
Sandwiches

<small>PREP: 25 MIN ▪ COOK: 6 MIN PER QUESADILLA ▪ 4 SERVINGS</small>

2 teaspoons vegetable oil

1 pound boneless, skinless chicken breasts

1/4 cup chopped fresh cilantro

1/4 teaspoon ground cumin

8 flour tortillas (8 to 10 inches in diameter)

Cooking spray

1 cup shredded Monterey Jack cheese (4 ounces)

1 can (4 ounces) chopped green chilies, drained

Salsa, if desired

Heat 2 teaspoons oil in 10-inch nonstick skillet over medium-high heat. Cook chicken, cilantro and cumin in oil 15 to 20 minutes, turning chicken once and stirring cilantro mixture occasionally, until juice of chicken is no longer pink when centers of thickest pieces are cut. Shred chicken into small pieces; mix chicken and cilantro mixture.

Spray 1 side of 1 tortilla with cooking spray; place sprayed side down in same skillet. Layer with one-fourth of the chicken mixture, 1/4 cup of the cheese and one-fourth of the chilies to within 1/2 inch of edge of tortilla. Top with another tortilla; spray top of tortilla with cooking spray.

Cook over medium-high heat 4 to 6 minutes, turning after 2 minutes, until light golden brown. Repeat with remaining tortillas, chicken mixture, cheese and chilies. Cut quesadillas into wedges. Serve with salsa.

1 Serving: Calories 495 (Calories from Fat 180); Fat 20g (Saturated 7g); Cholesterol 75mg; Sodium 690mg; Carbohydrate 50g (Dietary Fiber 3g); Protein 32g
*% **Daily Value:** Vitamin A 10%; Vitamin C 32%; Calcium 32%; Iron 20%*
***Diet Exchanges:** 3 Starch, 3 Lean Meat, 1 Vegetable, 2 Fat*

Betty's Tip

For a super-quick side dish, combine hot cooked rice with salsa or with melted process cheese spread. Top with sliced ripe olives and chopped green onions for a festive look.

Chicken Gyro *Wrap*

PREP: 8 MIN ▪ 4 SANDWICHES

1 1/2 cups chopped cooked chicken

1/2 cup chopped lettuce

1/4 cup diced red onion

1 medium cucumber, finely chopped (1 cup)

4 flour tortillas (8 to 10 inches in diameter)

8 tablespoons cucumber ranch dressing

Mix chicken, lettuce, onion and cucumber. Divide chicken mixture among tortillas, spreading to within 2 inches of bottom of each tortilla. Top each with 2 tablespoons dressing.

Fold one end of tortilla up about 1 inch over filling; fold right and left sides over folded end, overlapping. Fold remaining end down. Cut in half to serve.

1 Serving: Calories 405 (Calories from Fat 205); Fat 23g (Saturated 4g); Cholesterol 55mg; Sodium 470mg; Carbohydrate 31g (Dietary Fiber 2g); Protein 20g
% Daily Value: Vitamin A 2%; Vitamin C 6%; Calcium 10%; Iron 12%
Diet Exchanges: 2 Starch, 2 Lean Meat, 3 Fat

Try This

Increase the fun by trying other flavors of tortillas, such as red pepper, herb or tomato.

Adobe Chicken *Wrap*

PREP: 10 MIN ■ 6 SANDWICHES

1 1/2 cups chopped cooked chicken

1/2 cup salsa

1 can (15 to 16 ounces) black beans, rinsed and drained

1 can (7 ounces) whole kernel corn, drained

6 spinach or regular flour tortillas (8 to 10 inches in diameter)

1/3 cup sour cream

Salsa, if desired

Mix chicken, 1/2 cup salsa, the beans and corn. Divide chicken mixture among tortillas, spreading to within 2 inches of bottom of each tortilla. Top each with sour cream.

Fold one end of the tortilla up about 1 inch over filling; fold right and left sides over folded end, overlapping. Fold remaining end down. Serve with salsa.

1 Serving: Calories 335 (Calories from Fat 80); Fat 9g (Saturated 3g); Cholesterol 40mg; Sodium 640mg; Carbohydrate 50g (Dietary Fiber 7g); Protein 21g
% Daily Value: Vitamin A 4%; Vitamin C 12%; Calcium 12%; Iron 22%
Diet Exchanges: 2 Starch, 1 Lean Meat, 4 Vegetable, 1 Fat

Betty's Tip

Zest it up! Toss sprigs of fresh cilantro on top of the filling, then roll 'em up.

BBQ Chicken
Pizza

PREP: 8 MIN ▪ BAKE: 7 MIN ▪ 6 SERVINGS

3 packages (8 ounces each) Italian bread shells or 6 pita breads (6 inches in diameter)

3/4 cup barbecue sauce

1 1/2 cups cut-up cooked chicken

3/4 cup shredded smoked or regular Cheddar cheese (3 ounces)

6 tablespoons chopped red onion

Heat oven to 450°. Place bread shells on ungreased large cookie sheet. Spread barbecue sauce on bread shells to within 1/4 inch of edges. Top with chicken and cheese. Sprinkle with onion. Bake 7 to 12 minutes or until cheese is melted.

1 Serving: Calories 275 (Calories from Fat 70); Fat 8g (Saturated 4g); Cholesterol 45mg; Sodium 650mg; Carbohydrate 34g (Dietary Fiber 2g); Protein 19g
*% **Daily Value:** Vitamin A 6%; Vitamin C 4%; Calcium 12%; Iron 12%*
***Diet Exchanges:** 2 Starch, 2 Lean Meat*

Betty's Tip

Why not pick up some coleslaw at your favorite deli or grocery store to serve with this western barbecue pizza?

Chicken-Pesto
Pizza

PREP: 10 MIN ▪ BAKE: 10 MIN ▪ 4 SERVINGS

1 package (16 ounces) Italian bread shell or ready-to-serve pizza crust (12 to 14 inches in diameter)

1 container (7 ounces) refrigerated basil pesto

1 cup chopped cooked chicken

4 roma (plum) tomatoes, chopped

1/4 cup oil-packed sun-dried tomatoes, drained and sliced

1 1/2 cups shredded provolone cheese (6 ounces)

Heat oven to 450°. Place bread shell on ungreased cookie sheet. Spread pesto evenly over bread shell. Top with chicken, tomatoes and cheese. Bake about 10 minutes or until cheese is melted.

1 Serving: Calories 800 (Calories from Fat 415); Fat 46g (Saturated 14g); Cholesterol 75mg; Sodium 1350mg; Carbohydrate 67g (Dietary Fiber 5g); Protein 34g
% Daily Value: Vitamin A 18%; Vitamin C 16%; Calcium 50%; Iron 32%
Diet Exchanges: 4 Starch, 3 Lean Meat, 1 Vegetable, 7 Fat

Betty's Tip

For a lower-fat version, try reduced-fat pesto and sun-dried tomatoes that aren't packed in oil, and decrease the cheese to 1 cup.

Hawaiian
Pizza

PREP: 5 MIN ■ BAKE: 10 MIN ■ 6 SERVINGS

1 Italian bread shell or ready-to-serve pizza crust (12 inches in diameter)

1 can (8 ounces) tomato sauce

2 cups cubed cooked chicken

1 can (8 ounces) pineapple tidbits, well drained

1 cup shredded mozzarella cheese (4 ounces)

Heat oven to 400°. Place bread shell on ungreased cookie sheet. Spread tomato sauce over bread shell. Top with chicken and pineapple. Sprinkle with cheese. Bake 8 to 10 minutes or until pizza is hot and cheese is melted.

1 Serving: Calories 420 (Calories from Fat 90); Fat 10g (Saturated 4g); Cholesterol 50mg; Sodium 780mg; Carbohydrate 59g (Dietary Fiber 3g); Protein 26g
% Daily Value: Vitamin A 6%; Vitamin C 6%; Calcium 16%; Iron 22%
Diet Exchanges: 3 Starch, 2 Lean Meat, 1 Fruit, 1 Fat

Betty's Tip

Crushed pineapple, very well drained, can be substituted for the pineapple tidbits.

Thai Chicken *Pizza*

PREP: 9 MIN ▪ BAKE: 20 MIN ▪ 6 SERVINGS

6 flour tortillas (8 to 10 inches in diameter)

2/3 cup peanut butter

1/4 cup soy sauce

2 tablespoons seasoned rice vinegar

2 teaspoons sugar

3 cups shredded mozzarella cheese (12 ounces)

2 cups chopped cooked chicken breast

1 bag (16 ounces) frozen stir-fry vegetables, thawed

Heat oven to 400°. Place 3 tortillas on large ungreased cookie sheet. Bake 5 minutes. Beat peanut butter, soy sauce, vinegar and sugar, using wire whisk, until smooth; spread over tortillas.

Sprinkle 1/4 cup of the cheese over each tortilla. Spread chicken and vegetables evenly over tortillas. Sprinkle with remaining 1 1/2 cups cheese. Bake 10 to 15 minutes or until pizzas are hot and cheese is melted. Repeat with remaining tortillas.

1 Serving: Calories 575 (Calories from Fat 270); Fat 30g (Saturated 10g); Cholesterol 70mg; Sodium 1560mg; Carbohydrate 39g (Dietary Fiber 5g); Protein 43g
% Daily Value: Vitamin A 16%; Vitamin C 20%; Calcium 50%; Iron 20%
Diet Exchanges: 2 Starch, 5 Medium-Fat Meat, 2 Vegetable

Betty's Tip

Purchased peanut sauce, found in the Asian-foods section of your grocery store, can be used in place of the peanut butter, soy sauce, vinegar and sugar. Use a scant 1 cup of purchased sauce.

Chapter 7

Soups, Chilies and Chowders

Chicken Noodle
Soup

PREP: 10 MIN ■ COOK: 15 MIN ■ 4 SERVINGS

1 tablespoon olive or vegetable oil

2 cloves garlic, finely chopped

8 medium green onions, sliced (1/2 cup)

2 medium carrots, chopped (1 cup)

2 cups cubed cooked chicken

2 cups uncooked egg noodles (4 ounces)

1 tablespoon chopped fresh parsley or 1 teaspoon parsley flakes

1/4 teaspoon pepper

1 dried bay leaf

3 cans (14 1/2 ounces each) ready-to-serve chicken broth

Heat oil in 3-quart saucepan over medium heat. Cook garlic, onions and carrots in oil 4 minutes, stirring occasionally.

Stir in remaining ingredients. Heat to boiling; reduce heat. Cover and simmer about 10 minutes, stirring occasionally, until carrots and noodles are tender. Remove bay leaf.

1 Serving: Calories 295 (Calories from Fat 100); Fat 11g (Saturated 3g); Cholesterol 80mg; Sodium 1490mg; Carbohydrate 21g (Dietary Fiber 2g); Protein 30g
% Daily Value: Vitamin A 50%; Vitamin C 8%; Calcium 6%; Iron 16%
Diet Exchanges: 1 Starch, 3 1/2 Lean Meat, 1 Vegetable

Betty's Tip

Although available fresh, most bay leaves sold in the United States are dried. Slightly bitter in flavor, this aromatic herb comes from the evergreen bay laurel tree, which is native to the Mediterranean area. Bay leaves are always removed from the food before serving.

Chicken and Root
Vegetable Soup

PREP: 15 MIN ▪ COOK: 30 MIN ▪ 6 SERVINGS

2 tablespoons margarine or butter

1 small onion, finely chopped (1/4 cup)

3 medium carrots, thinly sliced (1 cup)

3 medium parsnips, peeled and sliced (1 cup)

1 medium leek, sliced (2 cups)

7 cups chicken broth

1 cup uncooked rosamarina (orzo) pasta (6 ounces)

2 cups shredded cooked chicken breast

2 tablespoons chopped fresh or 2 teaspoons dried dill weed

1/2 teaspoon salt

Melt margarine in Dutch oven over medium heat. Cook onion, carrots, parsnips and leek in margarine, stirring occasionally, until carrots are tender.

Stir in broth and pasta. Heat to boiling; reduce heat to low. Cover and simmer about 15 minutes, stirring occasionally, until pasta is tender.

Stir in remaining ingredients. Cover and simmer about 5 minutes or until hot.

1 Serving: Calories 285 (Calories from Fat 70); Fat 8g (Saturated 2g); Cholesterol 40mg; Sodium 1520mg; Carbohydrate 34g (Dietary Fiber 5g); Protein 24g
% Daily Value: Vitamin A 54%; Vitamin C 12%; Calcium 6%; Iron 16%
Diet Exchanges: 2 Starch, 2 Lean Meat, 1 Vegetable

Spring Arborio Rice and Chicken Soup

PREP: 16 MIN ▪ COOK: 30 MIN ▪ 6 SERVINGS

2 tablespoons olive or vegetable oil

1 small onion, finely chopped (1/4 cup)

1/2 pound boneless, skinless chicken breasts, cut into 1-inch pieces

1 cup uncooked Arborio or other short-grain rice

6 cups chicken broth

1/4 cup chopped fresh mint leaves

3 tablespoons chopped fresh parsley

1 package (10 ounces) frozen green peas

Freshly grated Parmesan cheese

Heat oil in Dutch oven over medium heat. Cook onion and chicken in oil, stirring frequently, until chicken is no longer pink in center.

Stir in rice. Cook 1 minute over medium heat, stirring frequently, until rice begins to brown. Pour 1/2 cup of the broth over rice mixture. Cook uncovered, stirring frequently, until broth is absorbed. Continue cooking 15 to 20 minutes, adding broth 1/2 cup at a time and stirring frequently, until rice is creamy and almost tender and 3 cups broth have been used.

Stir in remaining 3 cups broth, the mint, parsley and frozen peas. Cook over medium heat about 5 minutes or until hot. Serve with cheese.

1 Serving: Calories 280 (Calories from Fat 70); Fat 8g (Saturated 1g); Cholesterol 25mg; Sodium 1110mg; Carbohydrate 36g (Dietary Fiber 3g); Protein 19g
% Daily Value: Vitamin A 4%; Vitamin C 6%; Calcium 4%; Iron 16%
Diet Exchanges: 2 Starch, 2 Lean Meat, 1 Vegetable

Betty's Tip

Arborio is an Italian rice that, like pasta, is cooked until al dente, meaning "to the tooth."

Lemony Chicken-
Lentil Soup

PREP: 12 MIN ▪ COOK: 55 MIN ▪ 6 SERVINGS

**1 tablespoon olive or
vegetable oil**

**1 medium onion, chopped
(1/2 cup)**

**3 medium carrots, chopped
(1 1/2 cups)**

**2 cloves garlic, finely
chopped**

**1 cup dried lentils
(8 ounces), sorted
and rinsed**

2 tablespoons tomato paste

**2 cans (14 1/2 ounces each)
ready-to-serve chicken broth**

2 cups cut-up cooked chicken

**2 tablespoons grated lemon
peel**

Heat oil in 3-quart saucepan over medium-high heat. Cook onion, carrots and garlic in oil, stirring occasionally, until carrots are tender.

Stir in lentils, tomato paste and broth. Heat to boiling; reduce heat to low. Cover and simmer about 40 minutes or until lentils are tender.

Stir in chicken and lemon peel. Cook about 5 minutes or until hot.

1 Serving: Calories 225 (Calories from Fat 65); Fat 7g (Saturated 1g); Cholesterol 40mg; Sodium 510mg; Carbohydrate 24g (Dietary Fiber 8g); Protein 24g
% Daily Value: Vitamin A 48%; Vitamin C 6%; Calcium 34%; Iron 4%
Diet Exchanges: 1 Starch, 2 Lean Meat, 2 Vegetable

Try This

You'll really like this fresh lemony lentil soup. For a fun color change, use pink lentils.

Italian Chicken and Bean Soup

PREP: 15 MIN ■ COOK: 25 MIN ■ 4 SERVINGS

1 tablespoon olive or vegetable oil

1/2 pound boneless, skinless chicken breast halves, cut into 1/2-inch pieces

1/2 teaspoon Italian seasoning

2 cans (14 1/2 ounces each) ready-to-serve chicken broth

2 cups water

1/2 cup uncooked small pasta shells

1/2 cup uncooked juniorettes (small spiral pasta)

1 can (15 to 16 ounces) kidney beans, rinsed and drained

1 small red bell pepper, coarsely chopped (1/2 cup)

1 medium zucchini, cut into 1-inch pieces (2 cups)

Heat oil in 3-quart saucepan over medium-high heat. Add chicken; sprinkle with 1/4 teaspoon of the Italian seasoning. Cook, stirring frequently, 3 to 5 minutes or until browned.

Add broth and water. Heat to boiling. Add pasta, kidney beans and bell pepper. Heat to boiling; reduce heat. Cook uncovered 10 to 12 minutes, stirring occasionally, until pasta is tender. Stir in remaining 1/4 teaspoon Italian seasoning and the zucchini. Cook 3 to 5 minutes or until zucchini is crisp-tender.

1 Serving: Calories 375 (Calories from fat 70); Fat 8g (Saturated 1g); Cholesterol 35mg; Sodium 1400mg; Carbohydrate 53g (Dietary Fiber 9g); Protein 31g
% Daily Value: Vitamin A 12%; Vitamin C 34%; Calcium 6%; Iron 30%
Diet Exchanges: 3 Starch, 3 Very Lean meat, 1 Vegetable, 1 Fat

Try This

Use whatever pasta you have on hand that is similar in shape to the small shell or juniorettes pasta. If you use larger pasta, check the package directions for the cooking time.

Italian Chicken-
Lentil Soup

PREP: 15 MIN ▪ COOK: 40 MIN ▪ 6 SERVINGS

1 tablespoon olive or vegetable oil

1 pound boneless, skinless chicken breasts, cut into 1-inch pieces

1 medium onion, chopped (1/2 cup)

2 medium yellow summer squash, diced (2 cups)

4 medium carrots, thinly sliced (2 cups)

1 cup sliced mushrooms (3 ounces)

1 cup dried lentils (8 ounces), sorted and rinsed

1/4 cup chopped fresh or 1 tablespoon dried basil leaves

4 1/2 cups chicken broth

1/2 teaspoon salt

1/4 teaspoon pepper

1 can (28 ounces) Italian-style pear-shaped tomatoes, undrained

Shredded Parmesan cheese

Heat oil in Dutch oven over medium-high heat. Cook chicken and onion in oil 10 to 12 minutes, stirring occasionally, until chicken is no longer pink in center.

Stir in remaining ingredients except cheese, breaking up tomatoes. Heat to boiling, stirring occasionally; reduce heat to medium-low. Cover and cook 20 to 25 minutes or until lentils are tender. Serve with cheese.

1 Serving: Calories 260 (Calories from 55); Fat 6g (Saturated 1g); Cholesterol 45mg; Sodium 1230mg; Carbohydrate 32g (Dietary Fiber 11g); Protein 31g
% Daily Value: Vitamin A 74%; Vitamin C 26%; Calcium 10%; Iron 30%
Diet Exchanges: 1 Starch, 3 Very Lean Meat, 3 Vegetable

Betty's Tip

Lentils can be stored in a cool, dry place for up to 2 years. Lentils do not require soaking, and compared to other legumes, they cook in a relatively short time.

Tuscan Tomato *Soup*

PREP: 28 MIN ■ COOK: 30 MIN ■ 4 SERVINGS

2 tablespoons margarine or butter

1 medium onion, finely chopped (1/2 cup)

2 medium carrots, finely chopped (1/2 cup)

1 cup shredded cooked chicken breast

1/4 cup chopped fresh basil leaves

2 tablespoons sugar

1 teaspoon salt

10 large tomatoes, peeled and coarsely chopped (10 cups)

1 can (8 ounces) tomato sauce

Sliced fresh basil leaves, if desired

Melt margarine in Dutch oven over medium-high heat. Cook onion and carrots in margarine about 5 minutes, stirring occasionally, until onion is tender.

Stir in chicken, 1/4 cup basil, the sugar, salt, tomatoes and tomato sauce. Heat to boiling; reduce heat to low. Simmer uncovered 20 to 25 minutes, stirring occasionally, until flavors are blended. Serve topped with basil.

1 Serving: Calories 210 (Calories from Fat 80); Fat 9g (Saturated 2g); Cholesterol 30mg; Sodium 1080mg; Carbohydrate 33g (Dietary Fiber 7g); Protein 15g
% Daily Value: Vitamin A 100%; Vitamin C 60%; Calcium 6%; Iron 14%
Diet Exchanges: 1 Lean Meat, 6 Vegetable, 1 Fat

Betty's Tip

To save time in your busy schedule, use your food processor to chop the onion, carrots, basil and tomatoes.

Summertime Chicken *Gazpacho*

PREP: 25 MIN ▪ CHILL: 1 HR ▪ 8 SERVINGS

3 slices white bread, crusts removed

3 cloves garlic

2 tablespoons lemon juice

10 medium unpeeled tomatoes, diced (7 1/2 cups)

6 medium green onions, finely chopped (6 tablespoons)

2 medium cucumbers, peeled and diced (2 cups)

2 medium red bell peppers, diced (2 cups)

1 can (46 ounces) spicy eight-vegetable juice

2 tablespoons balsamic vinegar

1/2 teaspoon salt

1 cup cubed cooked chicken

Croutons, if desired

Place bread, garlic and lemon juice in a food processor or blender. Cover and process until bread forms fine crumbs.

Place bread crumb mixture in large bowl. Stir in remaining ingredients except chicken and croutons. Place half of the bread crumbs and vegetable mixture (about 7 cups) in food processor or blender. Cover and process until smooth. Repeat in small batches if necesssary.

Stir smooth vegetable mixture into vegetable mixture remaining in bowl. Stir in chicken. Cover and refrigerate at least 1 hour until chilled. Serve with croutons.

1 Serving: Calories 125 (Calories from Fat 20); Fat 2g (Saturated 0g); Cholesterol 15mg; Sodium 680mg; Carbohydrate 23g (Dietary Fiber 5g); Protein 9g
% Daily Value: Vitamin A 44%; Vitamin C 100%; Calcium 6%; Iron 12%
Diet Exchanges: 5 Vegetables

Buffalo Chicken *Chili*

PREP: 15 MIN ▪ COOK: 30 MIN ▪ 4 SERVINGS

1 tablespoon vegetable oil

1 large onion, chopped
(1 cup)

1 medium red or yellow bell
pepper, chopped (1 cup)

2 cups cubed cooked chicken

1 cup chicken broth

1 tablespoon chili powder

5 to 6 drops red pepper
sauce

2 cans (15 to 16 ounces)
pinto beans, drained

1 can (28 ounces) crushed
tomatoes, undrained

1 can (15 ounces) tomato
sauce with tomato bits

1/4 cup sliced celery

1/4 cup crumbled blue
cheese

Heat oil in 3-quart saucepan over medium-high heat. Cook onion and bell pepper in oil about 5 minutes, stirring occasionally, until crisp-tender.

Stir in remaining ingredients except blue cheese and celery. Heat to boiling; reduce heat to medium-low. Simmer uncovered 10 to 15 minutes, stirring occasionally. Serve topped with celery and blue cheese.

1 Serving: Calories 540 (Calories from Fat 155); Fat 17g (Saturated 5g); Cholesterol 65mg; Sodium 1760mg; Carbohydrate 78g (Dietary Fiber 24g); Protein 43g
% Daily Value: Vitamin A 50%; Vitamin C 90%; Calcium 24%; Iron 50%
Diet Exchanges: 4 Starch, 3 Lean Meat, 3 Vegetable, 1 Fat

Southwest Chicken and Chili Stew

PREP: 15 MIN ■ COOK: 40 MIN ■ 4 SERVINGS

2 1/4 cups chicken broth

1 pound boneless, skinless chicken breasts, cut into 1-inch cubes

4 cloves garlic, finely chopped

1 to 2 medium jalapeño chilies, seeded and diced

2 teaspoons all-purpose flour

1 medium red bell pepper, diced (1 cup)

1 medium carrot, sliced (1/2 cup)

1 cup whole kernel corn

2 tablespoons finely chopped fresh cilantro

1/2 teaspoon ground cumin

1/4 teaspoon salt

1/4 teaspoon pepper

1 teaspoon cornstarch

1/4 cup cold water

12 tortilla chips, coarsely crushed

Heat 1/2 cup of the broth to boiling in Dutch oven. Cook chicken in broth about 5 minutes, stirring occasionally, until white. Remove chicken from broth with slotted spoon.

Cook garlic and chilies in broth in Dutch oven over medium-high heat 2 minutes, stirring frequently. Stir in flour; reduce heat to low. Cook 2 minutes, stirring constantly. Gradually stir in remaining 1 3/4 cups broth.

Stir in chicken and remaining ingredients except cornstarch, water and tortilla chips. Heat to boiling heat; reduce heat. Cover and simmer about 20 minutes, stirring occasionally, until chicken is no longer pink in center.

Mix cornstarch and cold water; stir into stew. Heat to boiling, stirring frequently. Serve sprinkled with tortilla chips.

1 Serving: Calories 200 (Calories from Fat 45); Fat 5g (Saturated 1g); Cholesterol 50mg; Sodium 830mg; Carbohydrate 18g (Dietary Fiber 2g); Protein 29g
% Daily Value: Vitamin A 38%; Vitamin C 42%; Calcium 2%; Iron 8%
Diet Exchanges: 1 Starch, 2 Lean Meat, 1 Vegetable

Betty's Tip

Serve this colorful chili with cornmeal muffins and honey butter. To make your own honey butter, stir together equal parts of softened butter and honey.

White Bean
Chili

PREP: 10 MIN ▪ COOK: 20 MIN ▪ 6 SERVINGS

1/4 cup margarine or butter

1 large onion, chopped (1 cup)

1 clove garlic, finely chopped

4 cups 1/2-inch cubes cooked chicken

3 cups chicken broth

2 tablespoons chopped fresh cilantro

1 tablespoon dried basil leaves

2 teaspoons ground red chilies or chili powder

1/4 teaspoon ground cloves

2 cans (15 to 16 ounces each) great northern beans, undrained

1 medium tomato, chopped (3/4 cup)

Blue or yellow corn tortilla chips

Melt margarine in Dutch oven over medium heat. Cook onion and garlic in margarine, stirring occasionally, until onion is tender.

Stir in remaining ingredients except tomato and tortilla chips. Heat to boiling; reduce heat. Cover and simmer 15 minutes, stirring occasionally. Serve with tomato and tortilla chips.

1 Serving: Calories 430 (Calories from Fat 145); Fat 16g (Saturated 4g); Cholesterol 80mg; Sodium 710mg; Carbohydrate 39g (Dietary Fiber 10g); Protein 43g
% Daily Value: Vitamin A 14%; Vitamin C 2%; Calcium 16%; Iron 38%
Diet Exchanges: 2 Starch, 4 1/2 Lean Meat, 2 Vegetable

Betty's Tip

Ground red chilies are pure chili powder made from finely ground dried red chilies and containing no other ingredients. Chili powder starts with ground red chilies but also has cumin and oregano, and it may include paprika, coriander and salt.

Turkey-Corn *Chowder*

PREP: 15 MIN ▪ COOK: 37 MIN ▪ 6 SERVINGS

1 tablespoon vegetable oil

**1 pound turkey breast ten-
derloins, cut into 1-inch
pieces**

1 cup sliced leeks

1 clove garlic, finely chopped

**1/4 cup chopped fresh or
1 tablespoon dried dill weed**

1/2 teaspoon salt

1/4 teaspoon pepper

1 cup chicken broth

**3/4 pound small red pota-
toes, cut into 1-inch pieces**

2 cups half-and-half

1 cup julienne strips zucchini

**1/2 cup fresh or frozen
whole kernel corn**

Heat oil in 3-quart saucepan over medium-high heat. Cook turkey, leeks and garlic in oil 10 to 12 minutes, stirring occasionally, until turkey is no longer pink in center.

Stir in dill weed, salt, pepper, broth and potatoes; reduce heat to low. Simmer uncovered 15 to 20 minutes or until potatoes are tender. Stir in remaining ingredients. Cook uncovered about 5 minutes or until hot.

1 Serving: Calories 250 (Calories from Fat 110); Fat 12g (Saturated 6g); Cholesterol 70mg; Sodium 440mg; Carbohydrate 19g (Dietary Fiber 2g); Protein 19g
% Daily Value: Vitamin A 8%; Vitamin C 10%; Calcium 10%; Iron 10%
Diet Exchanges: 1 Starch, 2 Lean Meat, 1 Vegetable, 1 Fat

Betty's Tip

Cut out about 9 grams of fat per serving by substituting fat-free half-and-half or a low-fat liquid nondairy cream for the regular half-and-half.

Chicken Cordon Bleu
Chowder

PREP: 10 MIN ■ COOK: 7 MIN ■ 4 SERVINGS

2 cans (19 ounces each) ready-to-serve creamy potato with garlic soup

I cup cubed cooked chicken breast

I cup diced fully cooked ham

I cup shredded Swiss cheese (4 ounces)

I tablespoon chopped fresh chives

Heat soup, chicken and ham in 3-quart saucepan over medium-high heat 5 minutes, stirring occasionally.

Slowly stir in cheese. Cook about 2 minutes, stirring frequently, until cheese is melted. Served topped with chives.

1 Serving: *Calories 440 (Calories from Fat 245); Fat 27g (Saturated 10g); Cholesterol 90mg; Sodium 1430mg; Carbohydrate 19g (Dietary Fiber 1g); Protein 31g*
% Daily Value: *Vitamin A 6%; Vitamin C 4%; Calcium 28%; Iron 6%*
Diet Exchanges: *1 Starch, 4 Lean Meat, 1 Vegetable, 3 Fat*

Betty's Tip

Chicken or veal cordon bleu is a traditional dish that combines Swiss cheese and ham rolled up in chicken breasts or veal. We have used this flavorful combination in a hearty chowder.

Chicken-Cheese
Chowder

Prep: 18 min ▪ Cook: 20 min ▪ 6 servings

2 tablespoons margarine or butter

1 small onion, finely chopped (1/4 cup)

1 1/2 teaspoons ground cumin

1/2 pound boneless, skinless chicken breasts, cut into 1-inch pieces

2 large sweet potatoes, peeled and cut into 1-inch pieces

1 can (14 1/2 ounces) ready-to-serve chicken broth

1/2 cup whipping (heavy) cream

2 teaspoons chili powder

1/4 teaspoon salt

1 can (16 ounces) cream-style corn

1 can (4 ounces) chopped green chilies, drained

1 cup shredded Monterey Jack cheese (4 ounces)

Chopped fresh cilantro, if desired

Melt margarine in Dutch oven over medium heat. Cook onion, cumin and chicken in margarine 8 to 10 minutes, stirring occasionally, until chicken is no longer pink in center.

Stir in sweet potatoes and broth. Heat to boiling; reduce heat to low. Cover and simmer about 8 minutes or until potatoes are tender.

Stir in remaining ingredients except cheese and cilantro; cook until hot. Gradually stir in cheese just until melted. Sprinkle each serving with cilantro.

1 Serving: Calories 350 (Calories from Fat 160); Fat 18g (Saturated 9g); Cholesterol 65mg; Sodium 825mg; Carbohydrate 32g (Dietary Fiber 4g); Protein 19g
% *Daily Value:* Vitamin A 100%; Vitamin C 30%; Calcium 18%; Iron 10%
Diet Exchanges: 1 Starch, 1 1/2 Lean Meat, 3 Vegetable, 3 Fat

Try This

Sweet potatoes add color and a slightly sweet flavor to this chowder. For even more color, try yams.

Helpful Nutrition and Cooking Information

Nutrition Guidelines

We provide nutrition information for each recipe that includes calories, fat, cholesterol, sodium, carbohydrate, fiber and protein. Individual food choices can be based on this information.

Recommended intake for a daily diet of 2,000 calories as set by the Food and Drug Administration.

Total Fat	Less than 65g
Saturated Fat	Less than 20g
Cholesterol	Less than 300mg
Sodium	Less than 2,400mg
Total Carbohydrate	300g
Dietary Fiber	25g

Criteria Used for Calculating Nutrition Information

- The first ingredient was used wherever a choice is given (such as 1/3 cup sour cream or plain yogurt).

- The first ingredient amount was used wherever a range is given (such as 3 to 3 1/2 pound cut-up broiler-fryer chicken).

- The first serving number was used wherever a range is given (such as 4 to 6 servings).

- "If desired" ingredients (such as sprinkle with brown sugar if desired) and recipe variations were not inclued.

- Only the amount of a marinade or frying oil that is estimated to be absorbed by the food during preparation or cooking was calculated.

Cooking Terms Glossary

BEAT Mix ingredients vigorously with spoon, fork, wire whisk, hand beater or electric mixer until smooth and uniform.

BOIL Heat liquid until bubbles rise continuously and break on the surface and steam is given off. For rolling boil, the bubbles form rapidly.

CHOP Cut into coarse or fine irregular pieces with a knife, food chopper, blender or food processor.

CUBE Cut into squares 1/2 inch or larger.

DICE Cut into squares smaller than 1/2 inch.

GRATE Cut into tiny particles using small rough holes of grater (citrus peel or chocolate).

GREASE Rub the inside surface of a pan with shortening, using pastry brush, piece of waxed paper or paper towel, to prevent food from sticking during baking (as for some casseroles).

JULIENNE Cut into thin, matchlike strips, using knife or food processor (vegetables, fruits, meats).

MIX Combine ingredients in any way that distributes them evenly.

SAUTÉ Cook foods in hot oil or margarine over medium-high heat with frequent tossing and turning motion.

SHRED Cut into long thin pieces by rubbing food across the holes of a shredder, as for cheese, or by using a knife to slice very thinly, as for cabbage.

SIMMER Cook in liquid just below the boiling point on top of the stove; usually after reducing heat from a boil. Bubbles will rise slowly and break just below the surface.

STIR Mix ingredients until uniform consistency. Stir once in a while for stirring occasionally, often for stirring frequently and continuously for stirring constantly.

TOSS Tumble ingredients lightly with a lifting motion (such as green salad), usually to coat evenly or mix with another food.

Ingredients Used in Recipe Testing and Nutrition Calculations

- Ingredients used for testing represent those that the majority of consumers use in their homes: large eggs, 2% milk, 80% lean ground beef, canned ready-to-use chicken broth, and vegetable oil spread containing not less than 65 percent fat.

- Fat-free, low-fat or low-sodium products are not used, unless otherwise indicated.

- Solid vegetable shortening (not butter, margarine, nonstick cooking sprays or vegetable oil spread as they can cause sticking problems) is used to grease pans, unless otherwise indicated.

Equipment Used in Recipe Testing

We use equipment for testing that the majority of consumers use in their homes. If a specific piece of equipment (such as a wire whisk) is necessary for recipe success, it will be listed in the recipe.

- Cookware and bakeware without nonstick coatings were used, unless otherwise indicated.

- No dark colored, black or insulated bakeware was used.

- When a baking pan is specified in a recipe, a metal pan was used; a baking dish or pie plate means oven-proof glass was used.

- An electric hand mixer was used for mixing only when mixer speeds are specified in the recipe directions. When a mixer speed is not given, a spoon or fork was used.

Metric Conversion Guide

Volume

U.S. Units	Canadian Metric	Australian Metric
1/4 teaspoon	1 mL	1 ml
1/2 teaspoon	2 mL	2 ml
1 teaspoon	5 mL	5 ml
1 tablespoon	15 mL	20 ml
1/4 cup	50 mL	60 ml
1/3 cup	75 mL	80 ml
1/2 cup	125 mL	125 ml
2/3 cup	150 mL	170 ml
3/4 cup	175 mL	190 ml
1 cup	250 mL	250 ml
1 quart	1 liter	1 liter
1 1/2 quarts	1.5 liters	1.5 liters
2 quarts	2 liters	2 liters
2 1/2 quarts	2.5 liters	2.5 liters
3 quarts	3 liters	3 liters
4 quarts	4 liters	4 liters

Weight

U.S. Units	Canadian Metric	Australian Metric
1 ounce	30 grams	30 grams
2 ounces	55 grams	60 grams
3 ounces	85 grams	90 grams
4 ounces (1/4 pound)	115 grams	125 grams
8 ounces (1/2 pound)	225 grams	225 grams
16 ounces (1 pound)	455 grams	500 grams
1 pound	455 grams	1/2 kilogram

Measurements

Inches	Centimeters
1	2.5
2	5.0
3	7.5
4	10.0
5	12.5
6	15.0
7	17.5
8	20.5
9	23.0
10	25.5
11	28.0
12	30.5
13	33.0

Temperatures

Fahrenheit	Celsius
32°	0°
212°	100°
250°	120°
275°	140°
300°	150°
325°	160°
350°	180°
375°	190°
400°	200°
425°	220°
450°	230°
475°	240°
500°	260°

NOTE: The recipes in this cookbook have not been developed or tested using metric measures. When converting recipes to metric, some variations in quality may be noted.

Index

Note: *Italicized* page references indicate photographs.

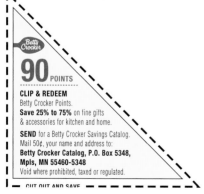

Moist Poultry Secrets

What is one of the biggest complaints cooks have about making chicken? It's too dry! Store-bought individually frozen or fresh chicken breasts have usually gone through a process in which the chicken was injected with a salt-water solution; these tend to be very tender, moist, juicy and are saltier. On the other hand, chicken breasts made without this process can be just a little less tender, moist and juicy. Whichever type you use, we offer you some great little secrets for moist and juicy chicken.

Secret #1

Wrap chicken tightly during storage to prevent it from drying out.

Secret #2

Marinating adds flavor and makes for juicy chicken. Marinate skinless boneless breasts for 1 to 2 hours and bone-in pieces up to 24 hours.

Secret #3

Brush chicken with milk, buttermilk, Dijon mustard or mayonnaise, then roll in bread crumbs, cracker crumbs or flour before cooking. The coating helps seal in moisture.

Secret #4

Cooking chicken with the skin on adds to the flavor, not the fat. Research has found that the fat does not transfer to the meat during cooking. So go ahead and leave the skin on—it helps keep the juices in, creates a moister, more tender meat and boosts the flavor. If you're watching your calories, fat and cholesterol, remove the skin after cooking and throw it away.

Secret #5

Don't overcook chicken or test too often for doneness. To test for doneness, use a knife to cut into the center of the thickest part of the chicken to see if the juice is no longer pink. Only test once or twice so the juices of the chicken stay in the chicken. Do not pierce the chicken with a thick, multi-tined fork or the chicken will lose an excessive amount of juice.

Secret #6

Don't undercook chicken either. Undercooked chicken will be tough and rubbery because it takes a certain amount of time and heat to soften the proteins in the chicken muscle.

Secret #7

Microwave chicken to partially cook it before grilling it. Not only does this save time, but it can also help prevent overcooked, burned chicken. To microwave, put the chicken, thickest parts to the outside edges, in a microwavable dish large enough to hold all the pieces in a single layer.

Cover with plastic wrap, folding back one corner to allow steam to escape. Microwave on High for about 4 minutes per pound, rotating dish after half the cooking time, until edges begin to cook; drain. Immediately put chicken on the heated grill and grill according to recipe.

Secret #8

Use tongs instead of a fork to turn chicken pieces in the skillet or on the grill. A fork will pierce the meat and let the juices escape.